Genres in Discourse

TZVETAN TODOROV
Directeur de Recherche, CNRS, Paris

Translated by Catherine Porter

CAMBRIDGE
UNIVERSITY PRESS

Published by the Press Syndicate of the University of Cambridge
The Pitt Building, Trumpington Street, Cambridge CB2 1RP
40 West 20th Street, New York, NY 10011-4211, USA
10 Stamford Road, Oakleigh, Melbourne 3166, Australia

First published 1990
Reprinted 1991, 1993, 1995

Printed in the United States of America

Library of Congress Cataloging-in-Publication Data
Todorov, Tzvetan, 1939-
[Genres du discours. English]
Genres in discourse / Tzvetan Todorov ; translated by Catherine
Porter.
p.   cm.
Translation of : Les genres du discours.
Includes bibliographical references.
ISBN 0-521-34249-X. – ISBN 0-521-34999-0 (pbk.)
1. Literature. 2. Discourse analysis. I. Title.
PN45.T57813   1990
801'.9–dc20
                                                        90-1663
                                                        CIP
British Library Cataloguing in Publication Data
Todorov, Tzvetan
Genres in discourse.
I. Title
801.4

ISBN 0-521-34249-X hardback
ISBN 0-521-34999-0 paperback

Contents

Prefatory Note

The texts that follow should need no special introduction here. Indeed, the first essay can be read as a project that the remaining texts pursue and exemplify. The first of the three groups of essays is general and theoretical in nature; in it the notions of literature, discourse, and genre are defined or discussed. The next section consists of studies in the two principal literary "genres," fiction and poetry; they deal with the shared problem of representation by means of language. The third section presents analyses of specific texts. These analyses are linked by a problematics common to language and the human mind: they take as their starting point the rejection of a certain idea of interiority, even a rejection of the inside/outside dichotomy. Although the essays are all rooted in the same set of preoccupations arising from the idea that literature is an exploration – the most intense exploration we know – of the powers of language, they were written separately, between 1971 and 1977; this may account for certain redundancies and inconsistencies. I have not sought to eliminate these systematically, judging that the process by which an idea is formulated and expressed may be (at least) as instructive as its simple statement.

As I reread these texts, I am struck by one feature about which the reader may well have some reservations: their "intermediate" character. I am not interested in speculation pure and simple, or in the description of facts as such; I continue to move between the two extremes. The entire field of literary theory has this intermediate status: it is challenged by a wholly general reflection on the one hand, and by the study of concrete texts on the other. The same ambiguity persists even in my writing style. I try to avoid both impressionistic writing – which I judge irresponsible, not because it is devoid of theory, but because it refuses to acknowledge theory – and terroristic formalism, where the author's sole object is to discover a more precise notation for an observation that is often quite imprecise in itself. I should like my discourse to remain permeable without becoming formless. Clearly, in trying to have it both ways, one risks losing on both counts: an unenviable fate, to which I shall nevertheless adhere.

PART ONE

1 *The Notion of Literature*

Before plunging into the abyss opened up by the question What is literature? I should like to offer a modest life preserver. My investigation will begin not with literature in its own right, but with discourse that, like my own, attempts to talk about literature. The difference lies in the itinerary rather than in the ultimate goal. Still, it seems possible that the path taken may be of greater interest than the destination.

We need to begin by casting doubt on the legitimacy of the notion of literature. The mere fact that the word exists, or that an academic institution has been built around it, does not mean that the thing itself is self-evident.

Reasons – perfectly empirical ones, to begin with – are not hard to find. The full history of the word *literature* and its equivalents in all languages and all eras has yet to be written, but even a perfunctory look at the question makes it clear that the term has not been around forever. In the European languages, the word *literature* in its current sense is quite recent: it dates back – just barely – to the nineteenth century. Might we be dealing with a historical phenomenon rather than an "eternal" one? Moreover, many languages (many African languages, for example) have no generic term covering all literary productions; and we are well beyond the days of Lévy-Bruhl, when this lack could be attributed to the well-known "primitive" nature of those languages, which were thought to be devoid of abstraction and thus also of terms designating genre rather than species. To these initial observations we may add the fragmentation characteristic of literature today. Who dares specify what is literature and what is not, given the irreducible variety of the writing that tends to be attached to it, from vastly differing perspectives?

The argument is not conclusive: a notion may legitimately exist even if there is no specific term in the lexicon for it. But we have been led to cast the first shadow of doubt over the "naturalness" of literature. A theoretical examination of the problem proves no more reassuring. Where do we come by the conviction that there is indeed such a thing as literature? From experience. We study "literary" works in school, then in college; we find the "literary" type of book in specialized stores; we are in the habit of referring to "literary" authors in everyday conversation. An entity called "literature" functions at the level of intersubjective and social relations; this much seems beyond question. Fine. But what have we proved? That in the broader system of a given society or culture, an identifiable element exists that is known by the label *literature*. Have we thereby demonstrated that all the particular products that take on the function of "literature" possess common characteristics, which we can identify with legitimacy? Not at all.

Let us use the term *functional* for our first approach to this entity, the approach that will identify it as an element in a larger system, through what this unit "does" in it. The second approach, in which we shall try to see whether all the instances of the entity that play the same functional role have the same properties, we shall call *structural*. The functional and structural viewpoints have to be rigorously differentiated, even though it is quite possible to pass from one to the other. To illustrate the distinction, let us consider a different object. Advertising unquestionably has a specific function in our society; but it becomes a much more complicated matter when we examine its structural identity. Advertising may use visual or auditory media, or others; it may or may not have temporal duration; it may be continuous or discontinuous; it may use mechanisms as varied as direct invitation, description, allusion, antiphrasis, and so on. For the undeniable functional entity (if we may take this at face value for the moment), there is not necessarily a corresponding structural entity. Structure and function do not imply each other in a rigorous way, even though it is always possible to observe affinities between them. This is a difference in viewpoint rather than in object. If we discover that literature (or advertising) is a structural notion, we shall have to account for the functioning of its component parts; conversely, the functional entity "advertising" is part of a structure that is, let us say, that of a society. The structure is made up of functions, and the functions create a structure; but since the point of view is what determines the object of knowledge, the difference is nonetheless irreducible.

The existence of a functional entity called "literature" thus by no means implies that of a structural entity (although it spurs us to try to find out whether or not such an entity exists). Now functional definitions of literature (by way of what it does rather than what it is) are quite numerous. We must not suppose that this path always leads to sociology: when a metaphysician such as Heidegger investigates the essence of poetry, he too grasps a functional notion. To say that "art is the enactment of truth"[1] or that "poetry is the foundation of being through language"[2] is to formulate a wish as to what art or poetry ought to be, without taking a position on the specific mechanisms that fit them for the task. The function may well be ontological; it remains a function nonetheless. Moreover, Heidegger himself acknowledges that for the func-

---

[1] Martin Heidegger, *Holzwege* (Frankfurt: Vittorio Klostermann, 1950) 25.

[2] Martin Heidegger, "Hölderlin und das Wesen der Dichtung," in *Erläuterungen zu Hölderlins Dichtung* (Frankfurt: Vittorio Klostermann, 1951) 38.

tional entity there is not necessarily a corresponding structural entity, since he tells us elsewhere that, in his research, "only great art is in question."[3] This does not give us an internal criterion that would allow us to identify any work of art (or literature), but only a declaration as to what one segment of art (the best part) ought to do.

The possibility exists, then, that literature may be nothing but a functional entity. But I shall not pursue this direction. I shall assume – at the risk of being disappointed in the end – that literature also has a structural identity, and I shall try to find out what this is. Many other optimists have gone before me, moreover, and I can use the responses they have suggested as a starting point. Without going into historical detail, I shall try to examine the two types of solutions that have been most frequently proposed.

A first definition of literature is based upon two distinct properties. Generically, art is "imitation," varying according to the material used; literature imitates via language, just as painting imitates by way of images. Specifically, art is not just any imitation whatsoever, for what is imitated is not necessarily real but may be fictitious, need never have existed at all. Literature is a *fiction*: this is its first structural definition.

The formulation of this definition did not take place overnight, and it has surfaced in quite varied terms. We may suppose that this property of literature is what Aristotle had in mind when he noted, first, that poetic representation parallels representation "by color and form," and, second, that "[the statements of poetry] are of the nature rather of universals, whereas those of history are singulars"[4]; this last observation makes more than one point. Literary sentences do not designate particular actions, which are the only ones that can really be produced. In another era, literature will be deemed fundamentally false, a tissue of lies; Frye has reminded us of the ambiguity of the terms *fable, fiction, myth,* which apply just as well to "literature" as to "falsehood." But this is unfair: literary sentences are no more "false" than they are "true." The first modern logicians (Frege, for example) noted that the literary text is not subject to the truth test, that it is neither true nor false but precisely *fictional*. This has become a commonplace today.

Is such a definition satisfactory? We may well wonder whether we are not about to substitute a consequence of what literature is for a definition of literature. Nothing prevents a story that recounts a real event from being perceived as literature. Nothing in its composition needs to be changed; we need only say that we are not interested in its truth value but are reading it "as" literature. A "literary" reading can be imposed on any text: the question of truthfulness will not arise *because the text is literary*.

Rather than a definition of literature, we are offered here, in a roundabout way, one of its properties. But can we observe this property in every literary

[3] Heidegger, *Holzwege,* 29.
[4] Aristotle, "De Poetica," 1447a, in *The Works of Aristotle,* vol. 11, ed. W. A. Ross, trans. Ingram Bywater (Oxford: Clarendon Press, 1924).

text? Is it a coincidence that we readily apply the word *fiction* to one component of literature (novels, short stories, plays), but that we use this label much less often, if at all, for another of its components, namely, poetry? We might be tempted to say that just as the novelistic sentence is neither true nor false even though it may describe an event, the poetic sentence is neither fictitious nor nonfictitious: the question does not arise, precisely inasmuch as poetry recounts nothing, designates no event, but confines itself, quite often, to formulating meditations or impressions. The specific term *fiction* does not apply to poetry because the generic term *imitation* has to lose all specific meaning if it is to remain pertinent. Poetry frequently evokes no external representation; it suffices in and of itself. The question becomes more difficult still when we turn to genres that are often termed "minor" but are nonetheless found in all the "literatures" of the world: prayers, exhortations, proverbs, riddles, nursery rhymes (each of which obviously poses different problems). Shall we declare that these too "imitate," or shall we remove them from the set of phenomena denoted by the term "literature"?

If everything ordinarily viewed as literature is not necessarily fictional, conversely not every fiction is necessarily literary. Let us take Freud's "case histories" as examples. It would be inappropriate to ask whether all the incidents in the life of little Hans or the Wolf Man are true. These incidents have quite precisely the status of fiction; all we can say about them is whether they serve Freud's thesis well or badly. Taking a completely different example, shall we include all myths within literature (given that they are undeniably fictional)?

I am not the first, of course, to question the notion of imitation in literature or art. Throughout the entire period of European classicism we can trace numerous efforts to amend it so as to make it serviceable, for it turns out that the "imitation" has to take on a very general meaning in order to embrace all the activities it is supposed to include. The term then applies equally well to a number of other things, however, and a complementary definition is required: imitation must be "artistic." But this amounts to using the term being defined in the definition itself. Somewhere in the eighteenth century, the situation is reversed. A new and entirely independent definition of literature appears, in lieu of adaptations of the old. Nothing is more telling in this regard than the titles of two texts that mark the boundaries of two periods. A text on aesthetics published by Charles Batteux in 1746 sums up the commonsense wisdom of the times: *Les Beaux-Arts réduits à un même principe.*[5] The principle in question is the imitation of beautiful nature. In 1785, another title echoes the first: Karl Philipp Moritz's *Schriften zur Ästhetik und Poetik* opens with an essay entitled "Versuch einer Vereinigung aller schönen Künste und Wissenschaften unter dem Begriff des in sich selbst Vollendeten."[6] The fine arts are

[5] Charles Batteux, *Les Beaux-Arts réduits à un même principe* (Paris: Saillant et Nyon, 1773).
[6] Karl Philipp Moritz, *Schriften zur Ästhetik und Poetik,* ed. Hans Joachim Schrimpf (Tübingen: Max Niemeyer Verlag, 1962) 3–9.

once again united, but now in the name of the beautiful, understood as an "achievement in itself."

The second great definition of literature, then, comes under the banner of the beautiful: here "pleasing" wins out over "instructing." Now the notion of the beautiful is crystallized, toward the end of the eighteenth century, in an affirmation of the intransitive, noninstrumental nature of the work of art. Having once been identified with the useful, the beautiful is now defined by its nonutilitarian nature. Moritz writes: "The truly beautiful consists in a thing signifying itself alone, designating itself alone, containing itself alone, in its being a whole accomplished in itself."[7] But art is defined in terms of the beautiful: "If a work of art has as its only reason for being the indication of something external to it, it would become by that very token an accessory; whereas in the case of the beautiful, the work of art is always primary."[8] Painting consists of images that are perceived for themselves and not in terms of some other purpose; music consists of sounds whose value lies in themselves. Literature, finally, consists of noninstrumental language whose value lies in itself, or as Novalis says, "expression for expression's sake." A detailed discussion of this reversal can be found in the central part of my book *Theories of the Symbol.*[9]

This position was defended by the German Romantics, who transmitted it to the symbolists; it came to dominate all the symbolist and postsymbolist movements in Europe. What is more, it became the basis for the first modern attempts to create a science of literature. Whether in Russian Formalism or in American New Criticism, the initial postulate is always the same. The poetic function is the one that focuses on the "message" itself. Even today this definition predominates, although its formulation may vary.

Such a definition of literature does not in fact deserve to be called "structural." It tells us what poetry has to do, not how poetry succeeds in carrying out its mission. However the functional tendency was complemented early on by a structural viewpoint. One aspect more than all the others leads us to perceive the work in itself, and that is its systematic character. Diderot had already defined the beautiful in this way; later on, the term *beautiful* was replaced by *form,* which in turn came to be replaced by *structure.* Formalist studies of literature have the merit (and this is how they establish the science of poetics) of being studies of the literary system, of the system of the work. Literature is thus a *system,* a language that attracts attention to itself through its systematicity alone, a language that becomes autotelic. This is its second structural definition.

Let us examine this hypothesis in turn. Is literary language the only systematic one? The answer is unquestionably negative. It is not only in realms customarily compared to literature – such as advertising – that we find rigorous

---

[7] Moritz, *Schriften,* 113.
[8] Ibid., 113.
[9] Trans. Catherine Porter (Ithaca: Cornell University Press, 1982).

organization and even the use of identical mechanisms (rhyme, polysemy, etc.); we also find these in realms that are, in principle, the most remote from literature. Can we say that juridical or political discourse is not organized, that it does not obey strict rules? It is not a coincidence, moreover, that until the Renaissance, and especially in Greek and Latin antiquity, Rhetoric went hand in hand with Poetics (we really ought to say that Poetics only came in on the heels of Rhetoric). Rhetoric had as its task the codification of the laws of nonliterary discourse. We could go further still and question the very relevance of a notion such as "system of the work," precisely by virtue of the great facility with which such a "system" can always be established. A language includes only a limited number of phonemes, and even fewer distinctive features; the grammatical categories of each paradigm are few in number. Repetition, far from being difficult, is inevitable. Saussure, as we know, formulated a hypothesis about Latin poetry according to which the poets wove a proper name into the text, the name of the person to whom the poem was addressed or about whom it had been written. His hypothesis leads to a dead end, not for lack of proof but rather because of an overabundance of proof: in any poem of reasonable length, we can find any name whatsoever inscribed. Besides, why limit ourselves to poetry? "This game was able to become the habitual accompaniment for any Latin writer of the form he gave to his thought the moment it sprang from his brain."[10] And why only the Romans? Saussure goes so far as to discover the name *Eton* in a Latin text that served as an exercise for the students at that college in the nineteenth century; unfortunately for him, the author of the text was a scholar at King's College, Cambridge, in the seventeenth century, and the text was not adopted at Eton until a hundred years later!

If it can be found so easily everywhere, such a system gets us nowhere. Now let us consider the complementary question. Is every literary text systematic enough to be called autotelic, intransitive, opaque? The meaning of such an assertion is easy enough to grasp when it is applied to a poem, an object "accomplished in itself," as Moritz might have said; but what about a novel? It is hardly my intention to suggest that the novel is merely a "slice of life" stripped of conventions, and thus of systematicity; but its system does not make its language "opaque." Quite to the contrary, the language of novels serves (at least in the classical European tradition) to represent objects, events, actions, characters. We cannot say, either, that the novel's ultimate goal lies not in language but in the novelistic mechanism. What is "opaque," in this case, is the world represented; but does not such a conception of opacity (or intransitivity, autotelism) apply just as well to any everyday conversation?

In our day, various attempts have been made to amalgamate these two definitions of literature. But since neither definition taken alone, is entirely sat-

---

[10] Jean Starobinski, *Words upon Words: The Anagrams of Ferdinand de Saussure,* trans. Olivia Emmet (New Haven and London: Yale University Press, 1979) 90.

isfactory, simply combining them can hardly advance our efforts. To correct the weaknesses of both definitions, it would be necessary to *articulate* them instead of simply adding them together or, worse, mixing them up. Unfortunately, the latter is what usually happens. Let us consider a few examples.

René Wellek deals with "the nature of literature" in a chapter of *Theory of Literature.*[11] He notes first of all that "the simplest way of solving the question is by distinguishing the particular use made of language in literature" (22), and he establishes three principal uses: literary, everyday, and scientific. Then he opposes the literary use in turn to each of the other two. As opposed to scientific usage, literary usage is "connotative," that is, rich in associations and ambiguous; it is opaque (whereas in scientific usage the sign is "transparent; that is, without drawing attention to itself, it directs us unequivocally to its referent"); it is plurifunctional: not only referential but also expressive and pragmatic (conative) (23). As opposed to everyday usage, literary usage is systematic ("poetic language organizes, tightens, the resources of everyday language") and autotelic, in that it does not find its justification outside itself (24).

Up to this point, we could take Wellek for a partisan of our second definition of literature. The emphasis on any particular function (referential, expressive, pragmatic) takes us far away from literature, where the value of the text lies in itself (this is what will be called the aesthetic function; Jakobson and Mukarovsky were already putting forward the same thesis in the 1930s). The structural consequences of these functional aims are a tendency toward system and the valorization of all the symbolic resources of the sign.

Another distinction follows, however, which appears to extend the opposition between everyday and literary usage. "The nature of literature emerges most clearly under the referential aspect," Wellek tells us, for in the most "literary" works, "the reference is to a world of fiction, of imagination. The statements in a novel, in a poem, or in a drama are not literally true; they are not logical propositions" (25). And here, he concludes, is the "distinguishing trait of literature," that is, "fictionality" (26).

In other words, without even noticing it we have moved from the second to the first definition of literature. Literary usage is no longer defined by its systematic (and thus autotelic) character, but by fiction, by propositions that are neither true nor false. Does this mean that the one is the same as the other? Such an assertion deserves at least to be formulated (not to say proved). We are no better off when Wellek concludes that all these terms ("organization, personal expression, realization and exploitation of the medium, lack of practical purpose, and, of course, fictionality" [27]) are necessary to characterize the work of art. The question we are asking is precisely what are the relations that unite these terms?

Northrop Frye raises the same issue in a somewhat similar way in *Anatomy*

[11] René Wellek and Austin Warren, *Theory of Literature,* 3rd edition (New York: Harcourt, Brace & World, 1956) ch. 2, "The Nature of Literature," 20–8.

of Criticism, in the chapter "Literal and Descriptive Phases: Symbol as Motif and as Sign."[12] He too begins by establishing a distinction between literary and nonliterary uses of the language (his nonliterary category subsumes Wellek's "scientific" and "everyday" uses). The underlying opposition turns out to distinguish external orientation (toward what signs are not) from internal orientation (toward the signs themselves, toward other signs). The oppositions between centrifugal and centripetal, between descriptive phase and literal phase, between sign-symbols and motif-symbols, are coordinated with the first distinction. Literary usage is characterized by internal orientation. We should note in passing that neither Frye nor Wellek ever asserts the exclusiveness of this orientation in literature, but merely its predominance.

Here again we encounter a version of our second definition of literature; and once more we glide toward the first before we know it. Frye writes: "In all literary verbal structures the final direction of meaning is inward. In literature the standards of outward meaning are secondary, for literary works do not pretend to describe or assert, and hence are not true, not false . . . In literature, questions of fact or truth are subordinated to the primary literary aim of producing a structure of words for its own sake, and the sign-values of symbols are subordinated to their importance as a structure of interconnected motifs" (74). In this last sentence, it is not transparence but nonfictionality (belonging to the true-false system) that is now opposed to opacity.

The operative term that makes this passage possible is the word *internal.* It appears in both oppositions, once as a synonym for *opaque,* and again as a synonym for *fictional.* Literary language usage is "internal," both in that the focus is on the signs themselves and in that the reality these signs evoke is fictional. Still, above and beyond the simple polysemy (and thus the basic confusion), perhaps each of the two senses of the word *internal* implies the other; perhaps every "fiction" is *opaque,* and every "opacity" *fictional.* This is what Frye seems to be suggesting when he asserts on the following page that if a history book were to obey the principle of symmetry (system, thus autotelism), by that very token it would enter the realm of literature, and thus of fiction. Let us try to see to what extent this two-fold implication is genuine; the effort will perhaps enlighten us as to the nature of the relation between our two definitions of literature.

Let us suppose that the history book obeys the principle of symmetry (and thus belongs to literature, according to our second definition); does it thereby become fictional (and thus literary according to the first definition)? No. We may have a bad history book, which is ready to twist the truth in the interest of symmetry; but the shift takes place between "true" and "false," not between "true/false" on one side and "fictional" on the other. Similarly, a political discourse may be highly systematic; that does not make it fictional. Is there a radical difference between a real account of a voyage and an imaginary travel

---

[12] Northrop Frye, *Anatomy of Criticism* (Princeton: Princeton University Press, 1957) "Literal and Descriptive Phrases: Symbol as Motif and as Sign," 73–81.

narrative in terms of textual "systematicity" (considering that the one is fictional and the other is not)? The focus on system, the attention paid to internal organization, do not imply that a given text is fictional. The implication does not work, at least not in this direction.

What about the other? Does fictionality necessarily involve a contextual focus? Everything depends on the meaning we give that last expression. If we take it in the restricted sense of recurrence, or of syntagmatic orientation (as opposed to paradigmatic), as some of Frye's remarks allow us to suppose, it is certain that fictional texts lacking in this property exist; the narrative may be governed entirely by the logic of sequence and causality (even though examples of this are rare). If we take the expression in the broader sense of "presence of any organization whatsoever," then all fictional texts possess this "internal orientation"; however we would be hard put to find any text that does not possess it. The second implication is thus not rigorous either, and it would be illegitimate to postulate that the two meanings of the word *internal* are the same. Once again, the two oppositions (and the two definitions) have been telescoped without being articulated.

We are left with the observation that the two definitions allow us to account for a large number of works ordinarily called literary, but not for all; and that the two definitions stand in a relation of mutual affinity, but not of implication. We remain floundering in imprecision and vagueness.

Perhaps the relative failure of my investigation can be explained by the very nature of the question I have raised. I have persisted in asking: What distinguishes literature from what is not literature? What is the difference between literary language use and nonliterary language use? Now by raising these questions about the notion of literature, I have been taking for granted the existence of another coherent notion, that of "nonliterature." Perhaps we need to begin by questioning this notion.

When the topic under discussion is descriptive writing (Frye), ordinary usage (Wellek), or everyday, practical, or normal language, a unified entity is always postulated which appears extremely problematic as soon as it is subjected to scrutiny. It seems obvious that this entity – which would include ordinary conversation as well as joking, the ritual language of administration and law as well as the languages of journalism and politics, scientific writing as well as philosophical and religious works – is not a single entity. We do not know just how many types of discourse there are, but we shall readily agree that there are more than one.

Here we have to introduce a generic notion, in relation to that of literature: the notion of *discourse*. This is the structural counterpart of the functional concept of (language) "use." Why is it necessary? Because, starting from vocabulary and grammar rules, language produces sentences; but sentences are only the point of departure of discursive functioning. Sentences are articulated among themselves and uttered in a given sociocultural context; they are transformed into utterances, and language is transformed into discourse. Furthermore, discourse is not a single entity; it is multiple, in its functions as well as in its forms: everyone knows that one must not send a personal letter in the place of an official report, and that the two are not written in the same way. Any verbal property, optional at the level of language, may be made obligatory in discourse; the choice a society makes among all the possible codifications of discourse determines what is called its *system of genres*.

The literary genres, indeed, are nothing but such choices among discursive possibilities, choices that a given society has made conventional. For example, the sonnet is a type of discourse characterized by supplementary constraints governing its meter and its rhymes. But there is no reason to limit this notion of genre to literature alone; outside of literature the situation is no different. Scientific discourse excludes as a matter of principle any reference to the first and second persons of the verb, along with the use of tenses other than the present. Jokes follow semantic rules that are absent in other types of discourse, while their metric composition, not codified at the level of discourse, will be fixed in the course of a particular utterance. Certain discursive rules have the paradoxical feature that consists in abolishing a rule of the language; as Samuel Levin and Jean Cohen have shown, certain grammatical and semantic rules are suppressed in modern poetry. But from the perspective of the constitution of a discourse, it is always a matter of more rules, not fewer. The proof lies in the fact that in such "deviant" poetic utterances we can easily reconstitute the linguistic rule that has been violated: it has not been suppressed but rather contradicted by a new rule. The genres of discourse, as we see, depend quite as much on a society's linguistic raw material as on its historically circumscribed ideology.

If we recognize the existence of types of discourse, our question about literary specificity should be reformulated as follows: Are there rules that apply to all instances of literature (identified intuitively) and only to these? But when it is put this way, the question can only be answered in the negative, or so it seems to me. I have already mentioned a number of examples attesting to the fact that "literary" properties are also found outside literature (from puns and nursery rhymes through journalistic reporting and travel narratives to philosophical meditations); hence our inability to discover a common denominator for all "literary" productions (unless it is language use).

Things change radically if we turn, not to literature now, but to its subdivisions. We have no trouble spelling out the rules of certain types of discourse (this is what *Arts poétiques* have always done, confusing the descriptive and the prescriptive, to be sure); elsewhere the formulation is more difficult, but our "discursive competence" always makes us sense the existence of such rules. Furthermore, we saw that the first definition of literature applied particularly well to narrative prose, while the second applied well to poetry; perhaps we would not be mistaken to seek the origin of two such independent definitions in the existence of two very different "genres." Indeed, the literature that has been taken particularly into account is not the same in the two cases. The first definition starts from narrative (Aristotle speaks of epic and tragedy, not poetry), the second from poetry (as in Jakobson's analyses of poems): two great literary genres have been characterized in this way, each time in the conviction that literature as a whole was involved.

In just the same way, we can identify the rules of discourse customarily considered "nonliterary." I shall thus propose the following hypothesis: If one opts for a structural viewpoint, each type of discourse usually labeled literary has nonliterary "relatives" that are closer to it than are any other types of "literary" discourse. For example, certain instances of lyric poetry and prayer have more rules in common than that same poetry and the historical novel of the *War and Peace* variety. Thus the opposition between literature and nonliterature gives way to a typology of discourses. And in my conclusions about the "notion of literature" I rejoin the last of the classics and the first of the Romantics. Condillac wrote, in *De l'Art d'écrire*: "The more the languages that deserve to be studied have increased in number, the harder it is to say what one means by poetry, because each people creates a different idea of poetry. . . . The 'naturalness' proper to poetry and to each type of poem is a naturalness of convention [!] that varies too much to be defined. . . . It would be fruitless to try to discover the essence of poetic style."[13] And Friedrich Schlegel wrote in the *Athenaeum* fragments: "A definition of poetry can only determine what this must be, not what it has been or is in reality; otherwise it would be expressed in its briefest form: poetry is what has been called poetry at any time, in any place."[14]

The result of this investigative path may seem negative: it consists in denying the legitimacy of a structural notion of "literature," in contesting the existence of a homogeneous "literary discourse." The functional notion may or may not be legitimate; the structural notion cannot be. But the result is only apparently negative, for in place of literature alone we now have numerous types of discourse that deserve our attention on an equivalent basis. If the choice of our object of study is not dictated by purely ideological motives (which would then have to be made explicit), it is no longer legitimate to concern ourselves exclusively with the literary subspecies, even if our workplace is called a "department of literature" (French, English, or Russian, and so on). To quote Frye once again, this time without reservation: "Our literary universe has expanded into a verbal universe"[15] or, at greater length: "Every teacher of literature should realize that literary experience is only the visible tip of the verbal iceberg: below it is a subliminal area of rhetorical response, addressed by advertising, social assumptions, and casual conversation, that literature as

---

[13] *Oeuvres philosophiques de Condillac,* Georges Le Roy (Paris: Presses Universitaires de France, vol. 1, 1947 [coll. Auteurs Modernes, vol. XXXIII]), 609, 611, 606.

[14] Friedrich Schlegel, *Kritische Ausgabe* (Munich: Ferdinand Schöningh, vol. 2, *Charakteristiken und Kritiken I (1796–1801),* 1967) fragment 114, "Die Athenäums-Fragmente," 181.

[15] *Anatomy of Criticism,* 350.

such, on however popular a level of movie or television or comic book, can hardly reach. What confronts the teacher of literature is the student's whole verbal experience, including this subliterary nine-tenths of it."[16]

A coherent field of study, for the time being parceled out among semanticists and literary critics, sociolinguists and ethnolinguists, philosophers of language and psychologists, thus demands imperiously to be recognized; in it, poetics will give way to the theory of discourse and to the analysis of its genres. It is from this perspective that the following pages have been written.

[16] Northrop Frye, *The Secular Scripture: A Study of the Structure of Romance* (Cambridge: Harvard University Press, 1976) 167.

2 The Origin of Genres

To persist in paying attention to genres may seem to be a vain if not anachronistic pastime today. We all know that genres used to exist: in the good old days of classicism there were ballads, odes, sonnets, tragedies, and comedies; but do these exist today? Even the genres of the nineteenth century, poetry or novel (and these are no longer quite genres in our eyes), seem to be coming undone, at least in the literature "that counts." As Maurice Blanchot said of the undeniably modern Hermann Broch, "like many other writers of our time, he has been subject to that impetuous pressure of literature that no longer recognizes the distinction between genres and seeks to destroy their limits."[1]

It is even considered a sign of authentic modernity in a writer if he ceases to respect the separation of genres. This idea, whose transformations can be traced back to the Romantic crisis of the early nineteenth century (despite the fact that the German Romantics themselves were major builders of generic systems), has found one of its most brilliant spokesmen in our day in the person of Maurice Blanchot. More forcefully than anyone else, Blanchot has said what others have not dared to think or have not known how to express: today there is no intermediate entity between the unique individual work and literature as a whole, the ultimate genre; there is none, for the evolution of modern literature consists precisely in making each work an interrogation of the very essence of literature. Let us reread a particularly eloquent passage: "The book is the only thing that matters, the book as it is, far from genres, outside of the categorical subdivisions – prose, poetry, novel, document – in which it refuses to lodge and to which it denies the power of establishing its place and determining its form. A book no longer belongs to a genre; every book stems from literature alone, as if literature held in advance, in their generality, the secrets and the formulas that alone make it possible to give to what is written the reality of a book. It would thus be as though, the genres having faded away, literature were asserting itself alone in the mysterious clarity that it propagates and that each literary creation sends back, multiplied

[1] Maurice Blanchot, *Le Livre à venir* (Paris: Gallimard, 1959) 136.

– as if, then, there were an 'essence' of literature."[2] And elsewhere: "The fact that literary forms, that genres, no longer have any genuine significance – that, for example, it would be absurd to ask whether *Finnegan's Wake* is a prose work or not, or whether it can be called a novel – indicates the profound labor of literature which seeks to affirm itself in its essence by ruining distinctions and limits."[3]

Blanchot's statements seem to have the weight of self-evidence in their favor. A single point in his argument might give us pause: the privileging of the *here and now*. We know that every interpretation of history is based on the present moment, just as that of space starts with *here,* and that of other people with *I.* Nevertheless, when such an exceptional status – the culminating point of all history – is attributed to the *I-here-now,* one may wonder whether the egocentric illusion does not have something to do with it. (This delusion turns out to be a counterpart of what Paulhan called the "explorer's illusion.")

Moreover, in the very texts where Blanchot announces the disappearance of genres we find categories at work whose resemblance to generic distinctions is hard to deny. Thus one chapter of *Le Livre à venir* is devoted to the diary form, another to prophetic speech. Speaking of the same Broch ("who no longer acknowledges the distinction of genres"), Blanchot says that he "indulges in all modes of expression – narrative, lyric, and discursive" (141). Even more significantly, the book as a whole is based on a distinction between fundamental modes, the narrative and the novel: the narrative mode is characterized by the insistent search for its own place of origin – which the novel mode effaces and conceals. Thus "genre" as such has not disappeared; the genres-of-the-past have simply been replaced by others. We no longer speak of poetry and prose, of documentary and fiction, but of novel and narrative, of narrative mode and discursive mode, of dialogue and journal.

The fact that a work "disobeys" its genre does not mean that the genre does not exist. It is tempting to say "quite the contrary," for two reasons. First because, in order to exist as such, the transgression requires a law – precisely the one that is to be violated. We might go even further and observe that the norm becomes visible – comes into existence – owing only to its transgressions. Blanchot himself says as much: "If it is true that Joyce shatters the novelistic form by making it aberrant, he also hints that that form perhaps lives only through its alterations. It would develop not by engendering monsters, formless, lawless works lacking in rigor, but by provoking nothing but exceptions to itself, that constitute law and at the same time suppress it. . . . One has to think that every time, in these exceptional works where a limit is reached, the exception alone is what reveals to us that 'law' of which it also constitutes the unexpected and necessary deviation. It is thus as if, in novelistic literature, and perhaps in all literature, we could never recognize the rule except by the exception that abolishes the rule, or more precisely, dislodges the center of

[2] Ibid, 243–4.
[3] Maurice Blanchot, *The Space of Literature* (Lincoln: University of Nebraska Press, 1982) 220; see also Maurice Blanchot, *L'Entretien infini* (Paris: Gallimard, 1969) vi.

which a certain work is the uncertain affirmation, the already destructive manifestation, the momentary and soon-to-be-negative presence" (133–4).

But there is more. Not only because, in order to be an exception, the work necessarily presupposes a rule; but also because no sooner is it recognized in its exceptional status than the work becomes a rule in turn, because of its commercial success and the critical attention it receives. Prose poems may have been exceptional in the days of Aloysius Bertrand and Baudelaire; today, who would dare write a poem in alexandrines, in rhymed verses – except perhaps as a new transgression of a new norm? Have not Joyce's exceptional word plays become the rule for a certain modern literature? Does not the novel, however "new" it may be, continue to exert its pressure on works being written today?

To go back to the German Romantics, and to Friedrich Schlegel in particular, in his writings, alongside certain Crocean assertions ("each poem, *sui generis*"), we find passages that tend in the opposite direction, establishing an equivalency between poetry and its genres. Poetry has certain things in common with the other arts: representation, expression, effect on the addressee. It has language use in common with everyday and scholarly language. Only the genres are its exclusive property. "The theory of poetic types would be the doctrine of art specific to poetry."[4] Poetry is its own genres, poetics is the theory of genres.[5]

In the process of arguing the legitimacy of a study of genres, we have come across an answer to the question raised implicitly in the title: the origin of genres. Where do genres come from? Quite simply from other genres. A new genre is always the transformation of an earlier one, or of several: by inversion, by displacement, by combination. Today's "text" (which is also a genre, in one of its senses) owes as much to nineteenth-century "poetry" as to the "novel," just as *"la comédie larmoyante"* combined features of the comedy and the tragedy of the previous century. There has never been a literature without genres; it is a system in constant transformation, and historically speaking the question of origins cannot be separated from the terrain of the genres themselves. Saussure noted that "the problem of the origin of language is not a different problem from that of its transformation."[6] As Humboldt had already observed: "When we speak of primitive languages, we employ such a designation only because of our ignorance of their earlier constituents."[7]

[4] Friedrich Schlegel, "Gespräch uber die Poesie," in *Kritische Ausgabe,* vol. 2, 306.

[5] We find a similar declaration in Henry James, who as a theoretician belongs to the posterity of Romanticism: "'Kinds' are the very life of literature, and truth and strength come from the complete recognition of them, from abounding to the utmost in their respective senses and sinking deep into their consistency" (Preface to *The Awkward Age,* in *Henry James: Literary Criticism* [New York: Literary Classics of the United States, 1984] 1131).

[6] Cited in Robert Godel, *Les Sources manuscrites du Cours de Linguistique générale de F. de Saussure* (Geneva: E. Droz, 1957) 270.

[7] Wilhelm von Humboldt, *Linguistic Variability and Intellectual Development,* trans.

The question of origin that I should like to raise, however, is not historical but systematic in nature; both questions seem to me equally legitimate, equally necessary. Not "what preceded the genres in time?" but "what presides over the birth of a genre, at any time?" More precisely, is there such a thing, in language (since we are dealing here with genres within discourse) as forms which, while they may foreshadow genres, are not yet included within them? And if so, how does the passage from the one to the other come about? In order to try to answer these questions, we must begin by asking just what a genre is.

At first glance, the answer seems self-evident: genres are classes of texts. But such a definition barely conceals its tautological nature behind the plurality of terms called into play: genres are classes, literature is textual. Rather than multiplying labels, then, we need to examine the content of these concepts.

Let us begin with the concept of *text,* or (to offer yet another synonym) *discourse.* We shall be told that discourse is a sequence of sentences. And here is where the first misunderstanding begins.

Where the acquisition of knowledge is concerned, an elementary truth is too often forgotten: that the viewpoint chosen by the observer reconfigures and redefines his object. So it is with language: one tends to forget that the linguist has a viewpoint from which she marks out an object, within the language material, that belongs to her; now this object will be altered if the viewpoint changes, even if the material remains the same.

A sentence is a unit belonging to language, and to the linguist. A sentence is a combination of possible words, not a concrete utterance. The same sentence may be uttered in various circumstances; for the linguist, its identity will not change even if, by virtue of altered circumstances, it changes meaning.

Discourse is not made up of sentences, but of uttered sentences, or, more succinctly, of utterances. Now the interpretation of an utterance is determined, on the one hand, by the sentence that is uttered, and on the other hand by the process of enunciation of that sentence. The enunciation process includes a speaker who utters, an addressee to whom the utterance is directed, a time and a place, a discourse that precedes and one that follows; in short, an enunciatory context. In still other terms, discourse is always and necessarily constituted by speech acts.[8]

George C. Buck and Frithjof A. Raven (Coral Gables: University of Miami Press, 1971) 21.

[8] This way of putting the problems is in no way original (the difference between sentence and utterance goes back at least to the distinction between grammatical signification and historical signification made by F. A. Wolf at the beginning of the century); I am only recalling the obvious, though this is sometimes neglected. For more thorough discussions using contemporary terminology, see the writings of Austin, Strawson, and Searle, or my own presentation of this problematics in *L'Enonciation* (*Langages* 17, 1970) and, in collaboration with Oswald Ducrot, in *Ency-*

Let us turn now to the other term of the expression "class of texts," that is, *class*. This term poses a problem only in that it is too easy to apply: it is always possible to discover a property common to two texts, and thus to put them together in a class. Is there any virtue in calling the result of such a combination a "genre"? I believe we will have a useful and operative notion that remains in keeping with the prevailing usage of the word if we agree to call genres only the classes of texts that have been historically perceived as such.[9] Evidence of such perception is found first and foremost in discourse dealing with genres (metadiscursive discourse) and, sporadically and indirectly, in literary texts themselves.

The *historical* existence of genres is signaled by discourse on genres; however, that does not mean that genres are simply metadiscursive notions and not discursive ones. As one example, we can attest to the historical existence of the genre known as tragedy in seventeenth-century France by pointing to discourse on tragedy (which begins with the existence of this word itself); but that does not mean that the tragedies themselves lack common features and that they could therefore not be described in other than historical terms. As we know, any class of objects may be converted into a series of properties by a passage from extension to comprehension. The study of genres, which has as its starting point the historical evidence of the existence of genres, must have as its ultimate objective precisely the establishment of these properties.[10]

Genres are thus entities that can be described from two different viewpoints, that of empirical observation and that of abstract analysis. In a given society, the recurrence of certain discursive properties is institutionalized, and individual texts are produced and perceived in relation to the norm constituted by

clopedic *Dictionary of the Sciences of Language,* trans. Catherine Porter (Baltimore: Johns Hopkins University Press, 1979). See also Dan Sperber, "Rudiments de rhétorique cognitive" *(Poétique* 23, 1975).

[9] This assertion has as its corollary the reduced importance that I am now granting the idea of theoretical genre, or type. I am not at all denying the need to analyze the genres in abstract categories; but the study of the possible types appears to me today to be a reformulation of the general theory of discourse (or of general poetics); the latter fully encompasses the former. The historical genres are theoretical genres; but to the extent that the converse is not necessarily true, the separate notion of theoretical genre seems to me to lose much of its interest, except perhaps within the framework of a heuristic strategy, as in the examples studied by Christine Brooke-Rose.

[10] I am ultimately more optimistic than the authors of two recent studies which helped me to clarify my own views (Dan Ben-Amos, "Catégories analytiques et genres populaires," *Poétique* 19, 1974, 265–86, and Philippe Lejeune, *Le Pacte autobiographique,* [Paris: Seuil, 1975] 311–41, "Autobiographie et histoire littéraire.") Lejeune and Ben-Amos are prepared to see an unbridgeable gap between the abstract and the concrete, between genres as they have existed historically and the categorical analysis to which they can be subjected today.

that codification. A genre, whether literary or not, is nothing other than the codification of discursive properties.

This definition in turn needs to be explained through the two terms of which it is composed: *discursive property* and *codification*.

Discursive property is an expression I take in an inclusive sense. It is common knowledge that, even if we do not restrict ourselves to *literary* genres, we find that any aspect of discourse can be made obligatory. Songs are different from poems by virtue of phonetic features; sonnets differ from ballads in their phonology; tragedy is opposed to comedy by virtue of thematic elements; the suspense narrative differs from the classic detective story by the way its plot is structured; finally, an autobiography is different from a novel in that its author claims to be recounting facts and not constructing fictions. To categorize these various types of properties (though the categorization is not particularly important for my purposes), we might use the terminology of the semiotician Charles Morris, adapting it to our own uses: these properties stem either from the semantic aspect of the text, or from its syntactic aspect (the relation of the parts among themselves), or else from the verbal aspect (Morris does not use this term, but it can serve to encompass everything connected with the material manifestations of the signs themselves). The difference between one speech act and another, thus also between one genre and another, may be situated at any of these levels of discourse.

In the past, attempts have been made to distinguish "natural" forms of poetry (for example, lyric, epic, or dramatic poetry) from its conventional forms (sonnets, ballads, odes), or even to oppose these two modes. We need to try to see on what level such an assertion may still have some meaning. One possibility is that lyric poetry, epic poetry, and so on, are universal categories and thus belong to discourse (which would not rule out their being complex – for example, they may be simultaneously semantic, pragmatic, and verbal), but then they belong to poetics in general, and not (specifically) to genre theory: they characterize possible modes of discourse in general, and not real modes of particular discourses. The other possibility is that such terms are used with regard to historical phenomena: thus the epic is what Homer's *Iliad* embodies. In the second case, we are indeed dealing with genres, but these are not qualitatively different on the discursive level from a genre like the sonnet (which for its part is also based on constraints: thematic, verbal, and so on). The most one can say is that certain discursive properties are more interesting than others: personally, I am more intrigued by the constraints that bear upon the pragmatic aspect of texts than by those involving their phonological structure.

It is because genres exist as an institution that they function as "horizons of expectation" for readers and as "models of writing" for authors. Here indeed we have the two sides of the historical existence of genres (some may prefer to speak of the metadiscursive discourse that has genres as its object). On the one hand, authors write in function of (which does not mean in agreement with) the existing generic system, and they may bear witness· to this just as well within the text as outside it, or even, in a way, between the two – on the book cover; this evidence is obviously not the only way to prove the existence of models of writing. On the other hand, readers read in function of the generic system, with which they are familiar thanks to criticism, schools, the book distribution system, or simply by hearsay; however, they do not need to be conscious of this system.

Genres communicate indirectly with the society where they are operative through their institutionalization. This aspect of genre study is the one that most interests the ethnologist or the historian. In fact, the former will see in a genre system first of all the categories that differentiate it from that of the neighboring peoples; correlations will have to be established between these categories and other elements of the same culture. The same is true for the historian: each epoch has its own system of genres, which stands in some relation to the dominant ideology, and so on. Like any other institution, genres bring to light the constitutive features of the society to which they belong.

The necessity for institutionalization makes it possible to answer another question we may be tempted to ask: even if we acknowledge that all genres stem from speech acts, how can we explain that not all speech acts produce literary genres? The answer is that a society chooses and codifies the acts that correspond most closely to its ideology; that is why the existence of certain genres in one society, their absence in another, are revelatory of that ideology and allow us to establish it more or less confidently. It is not a coincidence that the epic is possible in one period, the novel in another, with the individual hero of the novel opposed to the collective hero of the epic: each of these choices depends upon the ideological framework within which it operates.

We might establish the place of the notion of genre even more precisely by making two symmetrical distinctions. Since a genre is the historically attested codification of discursive properties, it is easy to imagine the absence of either of the two components of the definition: historical reality and discursive reality. In the absence of historical reality, we would be dealing with the categories of general poetics that are called – depending upon textual level – modes, registers, styles, or even forms, manners, and so on. The "noble style" or "first-person narration" are indeed discursive realities; but they cannot be pinned down to a single moment in time: they are always possible. By the same token, in the absence of discursive reality, we would be dealing with notions that belong to literary history in the broad sense, such as trend, school, movement, or, in another sense of the word, "style." It is certain that the literary movement we know as symbolism existed historically; but that does not prove that the works of authors identified with symbolism have discursive properties in common (apart from trivial ones); the unity of the movement may be centered on friendships, common manifestations, and so on. Let us allow that this may be the case; we would then have an example of a historical phenomenon that has no precise discursive reality. This does not make it inappropriate for study, but distinguishes it from genres, and even more so from modes, and so on. Genres are the meeting place between general poetics and event-based literary history; as such, they constitute a privileged object that may well deserve to be the principal figure in literary studies.

Such is the global framework of a study of genres.[11] Our current descriptions of genres may be inadequate; that does not prove the impossibility of a theory of genres, and the foregoing propositions are offered as preliminaries to such a theory. In this connection I should like to recall another fragment by Friedrich Schlegel, in which he seeks to formulate a balanced view on the question and wonders whether the negative impression one has when one becomes familiar with genre distinctions cannot be attributed simply to the imperfection of the systems proposed by the past. "Must poetry simply be subdivided? or must it remain one and undivided? or alternate between separation and union? Most images of the universal poetic system are still as crude and childish as those that the ancients, before Copernicus, made of the astronomical system. The customary subdivisions of poetry are only a static construction for a limited horizon. What one knows how to do, or what has some value, these are the immobile earth in the center. But in the universe of poetry itself nothing is at rest, everything is in the process of becoming and changing and moving about harmoniously; and the comets too have immutable laws of movement. But before the course of these heavenly bodies can be calculated, before their return can be determined in advance, the true universal system of poetry has yet to be discovered."[12] Comets too obey immutable laws . . . The old systems were capable of describing only the static result; we have to learn how to present genres as principles of dynamic production, or we shall never grasp the true system of poetry. Perhaps the time has come to put Friedrich Schlegel's program to work.

At this point we need to return to our initial question concerning the systematic origin of genres. It has already been answered, in a sense, since, as we have said, like all other speech acts genres arise from the codification of discursive properties. So our question has to be reformulated as follows: is there any difference at all between (literary) genres and other speech acts? Praying is a speech act; prayer is a genre (which may be literary or not): the difference is minimal. But to take another example, telling is a speech act, and the novel

[11] The idea that the genres can be associated with speech acts is formulated by K. Stierle, "L'Histoire comme Exemple, l'Exemple comme Histoire," *Poétique* 10, 1972, 176–88; Philippe Lejeune, *Le Pacte autobiographique,* 1975, 17–49, "Le pacte autobiographique"; Elisabeth Bruss, "L'autobiographie considérée comme acte littéraire," *Poétique* 17, 1974, 14–26. P. Smith examines genres from an ethnological viewpoint in "Des genres et des hommes," *Poétique* 19, 1975, 294–312; and Philippe Lejeune adopts a historical perspective in "Autobiographie et histoire littéraire," the concluding chapter of the book cited above (it contains further references on the subject). A. Kilito offers a list of genres characteristic of Arab literature, a list that emphasizes their relationships with speech acts: "We have requests that something be accomplished – a promise, for example, reproaches, threats, satire, excuses . . ." ("Le genre 'séance': une introduction," *Studia Islamica* 43, 1976, 27).

[12] *Athanaeum,* 434.

is a genre in which something is definitely being told; however, the distance between the two is considerable. Finally, there is a third case: the sonnet is surely a literary genre, but there is no verbal activity such as "sonneting"; thus genres exist that do not derive from a simpler speech act.

Three possibilities may be envisaged, in short: either the genre, like the sonnet, codifies discursive properties as any other speech act would; or else the genre coincides with a speech act that also has a nonliterary existence, like prayer; or else it derives from a speech act by way of a certain number of transformations or amplifications (this would be the case for the novel, based on the act of telling). Only the third case actually presents a new situation: in the first two cases, a genre does not differ in any way from other speech acts. In the third case, on the contrary, we do not take discursive properties as a starting point, but we start rather with other already constituted speech acts, in a progression from a simple act to a complex one. This third case, too, is the only one that warrants being set apart from the other verbal actions. Thus our question about the origin of the genres becomes the following: what transformations do given speech acts undergo in order to produce given literary genres?

I shall try to respond by examining some concrete cases. This procedural choice already implies that the question of the systematic origin of genres cannot be maintained as a pure abstraction, any more than genres themselves can be viewed either as purely discursive or purely historical phenomena. Even if the order of our discussion leads us from the simple to the complex, in the interest of clarity, the order of discovery follows the opposite path: starting from the observed genres, we are attempting to find their discursive origin.

My first example comes from a culture different from our own: that of the Lubas, inhabitants of Zaire. I have chosen it because of its relative simplicity.[13] "Inviting" is an extremely common speech act. The number of formulas used can be restricted; the result is a ritual invitation, such as is practiced in our society on certain solemn occasions. But among the Lubas a minor literary genre exists that is derived from the invitation, and which is practiced even outside its original context. In one example, "I" invites his brother-in-law to come into the house. However, this explicit formula appears only in the final lines of the invitation (29–33; the text obeys a metric scheme). The twenty-eight preceding lines contain a narrative in which it is "I" who goes to his brother-in-law's house, and the brother-in-law does the inviting. Here is the beginning of the narrative:

> I left my brother-in-law's house,
> My brother-in-law said: "Hello,"
> And I said: "Hello to you."

[13] I owe all my information about the literary genres of the Lubas and their verbal context to the generosity of Mme Clémentine Faïk-Nzuji.

> A few moments later, he said:
> "Come into the house," etc.

The narrative does not stop there; it brings us to a new episode, in which "I" asks for someone to join him in his meal; the episode is repeated twice:

> I say: "My brother-in-law,
> Call your children,
> So they can eat these noodles with me."
> Brother-in-law says: "Well!
> The children have already eaten,
> They have already gone to bed."
> I say: "Well!
> So that is the way you are, brother-in-law!
> Call your big dog."
> Brother-in-law says: "Well!
> The dog has already eaten,
> He has already gone to bed," etc.

Next comes a transition made up of proverbs, and at the end we arrive at a direct invitation, this time addressed by "I" to his brother-in-law.

Even without going into detail, we can observe that between the verbal act of inviting and the literary genre "invitation" of which the preceding text is an example, several transformations take place:

1. an *inversion* of the roles of sender and receiver: "I" invites the brother-in-law, the brother-in-law invites "I";
2. a *narrativization,* or more precisely, the embedding of the verbal act of inviting in the verbal act of telling; in the place of an invitation, we get the narrative of an invitation;
3. a *specification*: not only is someone invited, but he is invited to eat noodles; not only does someone accept the invitation, but he desires company;
4. a *repetition* of the same narrative situation, but one that includes
5. a *variation* in the actors who take on the same role: once it is the children, another time the dog.

This enumeration is not exhaustive, of course, but it may already suggest the nature of the transformations the speech act undergoes. They are divided into two groups that might be called (a) internal, in which the derivation takes place within the initial speech act itself (this is the case for the transformations 1, 3, 4, and 5); and (b) external, where the first speech act is combined with a second, according to a given hierarchical relationship (this is the case for transformation 2, where "inviting" is embedded in "telling").

Taking a second example, still within the same Luba culture, we shall begin with an even more essential speech act, that is, naming, attributing a name. In our culture, the meaning of personal names has generally been forgotten; proper names take on meaning by evoking a context or through association, not by virtue of the morphemes that constitute them. This can be the case for the Lubas; but alongside such meaningless names are found others whose meaning is fully contemporary and whose attribution, moreover, is motivated by the meaning. For example (I have not marked the tones):

> *Lonif* means "Ferocity"
> *Mukanza* means "Fairskinned"
> *Ngenyi* means "Intelligence"

Besides these names, which are essentially official, an individual may also receive more or less stable nicknames, whose function may be praise, or perhaps simply the identification of the individual through characteristic features, for example his profession. The elaboration of these nicknames already brings them close to literary forms. Here are some examples of one of these forms of nicknames, the *makumbu,* or praise names:

> *Cipanda wa nshindumeenu* – beam on which to lean
> *Dileji dya kwikisha munnuya* – shade in which to rest
> *Kasunyi kaciinyi nkelende* – ax that does not fear thorns

Such nicknames may clearly be considered expansions of proper names. In both cases, human beings are described as they are or as they ought to be. From the syntactic viewpoint, we move from the isolated noun (substantive or substantivized adjective) to a syntagma composed of a noun plus a relative clause that modifies it. Semantically, we move from words used in their literal sense to metaphoric expressions. These nicknames, like the names themselves, may also allude to proverbs or popular sayings.

Finally, among the Lubas there exists a well established – and well studied[14] – genre called the *kasala*. These are songs of variable dimensions (they may be eight hundred lines or more), which "evoke the various people and events of a clan, exalt with high praise its dead and/or living members and proclaim their great deeds."[15] Once again, then, we find a mixture of characteristics and praises: on the one hand, individual genealogies are indicated, one person being situated with reference to others; on the other hand, remarkable qualities are attributed to these individuals, the attributions often including nicknames like those we have just seen. Moreover, the bard calls upon individuals and instructs them to behave admirably. Each of these devices is repeated countless times. Clearly, the seeds of all the characteristic features of the *kasala* were already present in the proper name and even more so in that intermediate form, the nickname.

Let us now return to the more familiar territory of the genres of Western

---

[14] See Patrice Mufuta, *Le chante Kasàlà des Lubà* (Paris: Armand Colin, 1969); Clémentine Faïk-Nzuji, *Kasala, chant héroïque luba* (Lubumbashi: Presses Universitaires du Zaïre, 1974). For similar phenomena in Rwanda, see P. Smith, "Des genres et des hommes," especially pages 297–8.

[15] Nzuji, *Kasala,* 21.

literature, to try to see whether we can discover transformations similar to the ones that characterize the Luba genres.

My first example is the genre that I myself described in *The Fantastic: A Structural Approach to a Literary Genre.* If my description is correct, this genre is characterized by the hesitation that the reader is invited to experience with regard to the natural or supernatural explanation of the events presented. More precisely, the world described in these texts is indeed our own world, with its natural laws (these stories are not fairy tales), but within that universe an event occurs for which we have difficulty finding a natural explanation. What the genre encodes is thus a pragmatic property of the discursive situation: the reader's attitude, as prescribed by the book (the individual reader is free to adopt it or not). Most of the time the reader's role does not remain implicit but is represented in the text itself through a character who bears witness; the identification of the one with the other is facilitated by the attribution to that character of the narrator's function: the use of the first-person pronoun *I* allows the reader to identify with the narrator, and thus also with that witness who hesitates as to the explanation of the events that come to pass.

For simplicity's sake let us leave aside the three-way identification between the implied reader, the narrator, and the character who bears witness; let us acknowledge that we are dealing with an attitude on the part of the represented narrator. A sentence from one of the most representative fantastic novels, Potocki's *The Saragossa Manuscript,* sums up this situation emblematically: "I almost came to the conclusion that demons had taken possession of the hanged men's bodies in order to trick me."[16] The ambiguity of the situation is clear. The supernatural event is designated by the subordinate clause; the main clause expresses the narrator's adherence, but an adherence modulated by approximation. The main clause thus implies the intrinsic implausibility of what follows, and constitutes by that very token the "natural" and "reasonable" framework in which the narrator seeks to remain (and, of course, to keep the reader).

The speech act underlying the fantastic genre is thus, even if we simplify the situation a little, a complex one. Its formula might be rewritten as follows: *I* (a pronoun whose function has been explained) + verb of attitude (such as *believe, think,* and so on) + modalization of that verb in the direction of uncertainty (a modalization that operates along two principal lines: verb tense, here the past, which contributes to establishing a distance between narrator and character; and adverbs of manner such as *almost, perhaps, doubtless,* and so on) along with a subordinate clause describing a supernatural event.

In this abstract and reduced form, the "fantastic" speech act may of course be found outside literature: it is the speech act of a person reporting an event that falls outside the framework of natural explanations, when that person still does not want to renounce the framework itself, and thus shares his uncertainty

[16] Jan Potocki, *The Saragossa Manuscript: A Collection of Weird Tales,* ed. Roger Caillois, trans. Elisabeth Abbott (New York: The Orion Press, 1960) 122.

with us (the situation may be less common today but is in any event perfectly genuine). The identity of the genre is entirely determined by that of the speech act, which does not mean that the two are one and the same. This kernel is enriched by a series of amplifications, in the rhetorical sense: 1) a narrativization: a situation must be created in which the narrator ends up formulating our model sentence, or one of its synonyms; 2) a gradation, or at least an irreversibility in the appearance of the supernatural; 3) a thematic proliferation: certain themes, such as sexual perversions or states approaching insanity, are preferred to others; 4) a verbal representation that exploits, for example, the uncertainty one may feel in choosing between the literal and figurative meanings of an expression (I sought to describe these themes and devices in *The Fantastic*).

Thus from the perspective of origins, there is no difference in nature between the fantastic genre and those we encountered in Luba oral literature, although differences of degree – that is, of complexity – may remain. The verbal act expressing "fantastic" hesitation is less common than the act that names or invites: it is nonetheless a verbal act like the others. The transformations it undergoes to become a literary genre may be more numerous and more varied than those with which we have become acquainted in the Luba literature; they remain of the same nature.

Autobiography is another genre proper to our society that has been described in sufficient detail to allow us to examine it from our current perspective.[17] To put it simply, autobiography is defined by two identifications: the author's identification with the narrator, and the narrator's identification with the chief protagonist. This second identification is obvious: it is the one expressed in the prefix *auto-* and the one that makes it possible to differentiate autobiography from biography or memoirs. The first one is more subtle: it distinguishes autobiography (like biography and memoirs) from the novel, even though a given novel may be full of elements drawn from the author's life. In short, this identification separates all the "referential" or "historical" genres from all the "fictional" genres: the reality of the referent is clearly indicated, because we are dealing with the author of the book himself, an individual who has a civil status in his home town.

Thus we are dealing with a speech act that codifies both semantic properties (this is what is implied by the narrator-character identification; one must speak of oneself) and pragmatic properties (by virtue of the author-narrator identification; one claims to be telling the truth and not a fiction). In this form, the speech act is very widely distributed outside literature: it is practiced every time anyone *tells his or her own story*. It is curious to note that the studies by Lejeune and Bruss on which I am relying here, under the cover of a description of the genre, have in fact established the identity of the speech act that is only its kernel. This shift of object is revealing: the identity of the genre comes

---

[17] See in particular Philippe Lejeune, "Le pacte autobiographique," and Elisabeth Bruss, "L'autobiographie considérée comme acte littéraire."

from the speech act that is at its root, telling one's own story; however, this initial contact is not prevented from undergoing numerous transformations in order to become a literary genre (I shall leave the task of identifying these transformations to specialists).

What would be the situation with even more complex genres, such as the novel? I do not dare plunge headlong into the series of transformations that presides over its birth; but I shall risk betraying a certain optimism and say that, here too, the process does not seem to be qualitatively different. The difficulty of the study of the "origin of the novel" understood in this sense arises only from the infinite embedding of speech acts with others. At the very top of the pyramid, there would be the fictional contract (thus the codification of a pragmatic property), which in turn would demand an alternation of descriptive and narrative elements, that is, the description of immobilized states and actions taking place over time (it must be noted that these two speech acts are mutually coordinated and not embedded one within the other as in the preceding cases). To this would be added constraints concerning the verbal aspect of the text (the alternation of the narrator's discourse and that of the characters) and its semantic aspect (private life, preferably with sweeping period frescoes), and so on . . .

The rapid enumeration I have just proposed is in no way different, moreover – except perhaps in its brevity and its schematic nature – from studies that have been devoted to the novel. And yet that is not quite an accurate statement, for such studies have lacked the perspective – a minuscule displacement, an optical illusion perhaps? – that makes it possible to see that there is not an abyss between literature and what is not literature, that the literary genres originate, quite simply, in human discourse.

PART TWO

3 *The Two Principles of Narrative*

Since, we are about to take up the question of narrative, let me begin by telling a story.

Ricciardo Minutolo is in love with Filippello's wife Catella. Despite his best efforts, however, Ricciardo's love is not returned. When he discovers that Catella is extremely jealous of her husband, Ricciardo decides to take advantage of this weakness. After making a public display of his lack of interest in Catella, he finds an occasion to convey the same impression to her directly; at the same time, he informs her of approaches Filippello has purportedly made to his own wife. Catella is furious and wants all the details. Nothing could be easier, Ricciardo replies. Filippello has made a date to meet Ricciardo's wife the next day, at a nearby bath house; Catella has only to show up there instead, and she will be convinced of her husband's treachery. So Catella goes to the bath house – where she finds Ricciardo in her husband's place. She fails to recognize him, however, as the meeting place is completely dark. Catella cooperates with the desires of the man she takes to be her husband, but then immediately begins to reproach him, explaining that she is not Ricciardo's wife, but Catella. Ricciardo reveals in turn that he himself is not Filippello. Catella is distraught, but Ricciardo convinces her that scandal would be in no one's interests, and "how much more savoury a lover's kisses are than those of a husband."[1]

So all ends well, and Boccaccio adds that this tale was praised by all who first heard it.

The foregoing text consists of a sequence of propositions that is easily recognized as a narrative. But what *makes* it a narrative? Let us go back to the beginning of the story. First Boccaccio describes Naples, the setting for the action; next he presents the three protagonists; after that, he speaks of Ricciardo's love for Catella. Is that a narrative? Here I think we can readily agree that the answer is "no." This judgment does not depend on the dimensions of the text; the passage in question takes only two paragraphs in Boccaccio, but we sense that it could be five times as long without making any difference.

---

[1] *The Decameron of Giovanni Boccaccio,* trans. Richard Aldington (New York: Dell Publishing Company, 1982) 207, "Third Day, Sixth Tale."

On the other hand, when Boccaccio says: "Such was his state of mind when . . ." (and in the French translation there is a change of tense here from the imperfect to the *passé simple*), the narrative takes off. The explanation seems straightforward. The beginning of the text presents the description of a state of affairs. That does not suffice for narrative, however, as narrative requires the unfolding of an action, change, difference.

Every change constitutes in fact a new narrative link. Ricciardo learns of Catella's extreme jealousy – which allows him to conceive of his plan – after which he can carry it out – Catella reacts as Ricciardo had hoped – the meeting takes place – Catella reveals her true identity – Ricciardo reveals his – they discover their happiness together. Each action thus isolated follows the previous one and most of the time the two are in a causal relation. Catella's jealousy is a *condition* of the plan that is concocted; the plan has the meeting as a *consequence*; public condemnation is *implied* by adultery; and so on.

Description and narrative both presuppose temporality, but the temporality differs in kind. The initial description was situated in time, to be sure, but in an ongoing, continuous time frame, whereas the changes that characterize narrative slice time up into discontinuous units: duration-time as opposed to event-time. Description alone is not enough to constitute a narrative; narrative for its part does not exclude description, however. If we needed a generic term to include both narrative texts and descriptive texts (that is, texts containing only descriptions), we might choose the term *fiction* (the French cognate term is used relatively rarely). This would have two advantages: first, because fiction includes narration *and* description; second, because it evokes the transitive and referential use made of words in each case (and the texts of someone like Raymond Roussel, who bases narrative on the distance that exists between two senses of a given word, do not constitute counterexamples), as opposed to the intransitive, literal use that is made of language in poetry.

This way of looking at narrative as the chronological and sometimes causal linkage of discontinuous units is of course not new. Vladimir Propp's work on the Russian fairy tale, which leads to a similar conclusion, is widely known today. Propp uses the term *function* for each action isolated when actions are seen from the perspective of their usefulness to the story; and he postulates that for all the Russian fairy tales there are only thirty-one types of function. "If we read through all of the functions one after another, we quickly observe that one function develops out of another with logical and artistic necessity. We see that not a single function excludes another. They all revolve on a single pivot, and not . . . on a variety of pivotal stocks."[2] Functions come in sequence and are not alike.

Propp analyzes one tale, "The Swan-Geese," in its entirety; we shall summarize his analysis here. This is the story of a young girl who neglects to look after her little brother. The swan-geese kidnap him, the girl goes off to find him, and succeeds, thanks to the wise counsel of a hedgehog. She takes her

---

[2] Vladimir Propp, *Morphology of the Folktale*, ed. Svatava Pirkova-Jakobson, trans. Laurence Scott (Bloomington: Indiana University Research Center, 1958) 58.

brother away; the swan-geese set out in pursuit, but, with the help of the
river, the apple tree, and the woodstove, she manages to get him home safe
and sound. In this narrative Propp singles out twenty-seven elements, of which
eighteen are functions (the others are descriptions, transitions, and so forth)
belonging to the canonical list of thirty-one. Each function is situated on the
same level as, while being totally different from, all the others; one function
is related to another only through chronological succession.

The validity of this analysis can be questioned, particularly as regards the
possibility that Propp may have confused generic (and empirical) necessity
with theoretical necessity. All the functions may be equally necessary to the
Russian fairy tale; but are they all necessary for the same reasons? Let us try
an experiment. When I told the Russian tale, I omitted some of the initial
functions: for example, the girl's parents had forbidden her to stray from the
house; the girl had chosen to go off to play; and so on. The tale is nevertheless
a narrative, fundamentally unchanged. On the other hand, if I had not said
that a girl and a boy were playing at home, or that the geese had kidnapped
the boy, or that the girl had gone looking for him, there would have been no
narrative, or a different one. We may conclude that not all functions are
necessary to the narrative in the same way; a hierarchical order has to be
introduced.

If we analyze "The Swan-Geese" this way, we shall discover that the tale
includes five obligatory elements: (1) the opening situation of equilibrium; (2)
the degradation of the situation through the kidnapping of the boy; (3) the
state of disequilibrium observed by the little girl; (4) the search for and recovery
of the boy; (5) the reestablishment of the initial equilibrium – the return home.
If any one of these five actions had been omitted, the tale would have lost its
identity. Of course one can imagine a tale that omits the first two elements
and begins with a situation that is already deficient; or a tale might omit the
last two elements and end on an unhappy note. But we sense that these would
be two halves of the cycle, whereas here we have the cycle in full. Theoretical
research has shown – and empirical studies have confirmed – that this cycle
belongs to the very definition of narrative: one cannot imagine a narrative that
fails to contain at least a part of it.

The actions Propp identified do not all have the same status. Some are
optional, supplementary to the basic schema. For example, the little girl's
absence at the time of the kidnapping may be motivated or not. Other actions
are alternatives, of which at least one has to occur in the tale: these are concrete
realizations of the action prescribed by the schema. For example, the little girl
finds her brother thanks to the intervention of a helper; however, she might
just as well have found him owing to her speedy legs, or her divinatory powers,
and so forth. In his well-known book *La Logique du récit,* Claude Bremond
has taken up the challenge of cataloging the possible alternatives available to
any narrative whatsoever.[3]

But if the elementary actions are arranged hierarchically, it is apparent that

[3] Claude Bremond, *La Logique du récit* (Paris: Editions du Seuil, 1973).

new relations prevail among them: sequence and consequence no longer suffice. The fifth element obviously echoes the first (the state of equilibrium), while the third is an inversion of the first. Moreover, the second and the fourth elements are symmetrically opposed: the little boy is taken away from home and is brought back home. Thus it is incorrect to maintain that the elements are related only by *succession*; we can say that they are also related by *transformation*. Here finally we have the two principles of narrative.

Can a narrative dispense with the second principle, transformation? In discussing the problems of definition and denomination, we need to be aware of a certain arbitrariness that invariably accompanies these gestures. We find ourselves confronting a continuum of facts and relationships; we then establish a limit somewhere, and call everything on one side of the limit "narrative," and everything on the other side "nonnarrative." But the words of the language we use have different nuances depending on who is speaking. A moment ago I contrasted narration and description by way of the two types of temporality they exhibit; however, others would call a book like Robbe-Grillet's *Dans le labyrinthe* a narrative, even though it suspends narrative time and posits variations in the characters' behavior as simultaneous. The same can be said regarding the presence or absence of relations of transformation between individual actions. A narrative lacking in such relations can be constructed artificially; real examples of the pure logic of succession may even be found in certain chronicles. But we shall have no trouble agreeing, I think, that neither these chronicles nor Robbe-Grillet's novels are typical representatives of narrative. We may take this argument even further: by bringing to light the difference between narration and description, or between the principle of succession and the principle of transformation, we have made it possible to understand why we perceive such narratives as marginal, in one sense of the term. Ordinarily, even the simplest, least elaborate narrative puts the two principles into action simultaneously. As (anecdotal) evidence, let us look at the French title of a recent spaghetti Western: *Je vais, je tire, je reviens* ("I go off, I shoot, I come back"): the apparently straightforward succession obscures a relation of transformation between "going off" and "coming back."

What is the nature of such transformations? The one we have noted so far consists in changing some term into its opposite or its contrary; for simplicity's sake, we shall call it *negation*. Lévi-Strauss and Greimas have placed particular emphasis on this transformation. They have scrutinized its various manifestations to such an extent that one might conclude it is the only transformation possible. It is true that the transformation of negation enjoys a special status, no doubt owing to the privileged position occupied by negation in our system of thought. The passage from A to non-A is in a way the paradigm of all change. Still, this exceptional status must not be allowed to obscure the existence of other transformations – which are numerous, as we shall see. In the tale Propp analyzed, for instance, we can find a transformation of mode: the interdiction – in other words, a negative obligation – imposed upon the little girl by her parents (she was not to leave her brother's side for an instant). And there is a transformation of intention: the little girl decides to leave in search of her brother, then she actually leaves; the first action relates to the second as an intention to its realization.

Returning to our tale from the *Decameron,* we can see the same relationships there. Ricciardo is unhappy at the beginning, happy at the end: a transformation of negation. He wants to possess Catella, then he possesses her: a transformation of mode. But other relations seem to play an even more important role. A single action is presented three times: first of all, there is Ricciardo's plan for getting Catella into the bath house, then there is Catella's erroneous perception of that scene, when she thinks she is meeting her husband there; finally the true situation is revealed. The relation between the first and third propositions is that of a project to its realization; in the relation between the second and the third, an erroneous perception of an event is opposed to an accurate perception of that same event. This deception is obviously the key to Boccaccio's narrative. A qualitative difference separates the first type of transformations from the second. The first case involved a modification carried out on a basic predicate; the predicate was taken in its positive or negative form, modalized or unmodalized. Here the initial predicate turns out to be accompanied by a secondary predicate, such as "to plan" or "to learn." Paradoxically, this secondary predicate designates an autonomous action but at the same time can never appear all by itself: one always projects *toward* another action. The lineaments of an opposition between two types of narrative organization are beginning to take shape. On the one hand we have narratives in which the logic of succession and transformations of the first type are combined; these will be the simpler narratives, as it were, and I should like to use the term *mythological* for this type of organization. On the other hand, we have the type of narrative in which the logic of succession is supported by the second sort of transformation, narratives in which the event itself is less important than our perception of it, and degree of knowledge we have of it: hence I propose the term *gnoseological* for this second type of narrative organization (it might also be called *epistemical*).

It goes without saying that an opposition of this sort is not intended to result in the distribution of all the world's narratives into two piles, with mythological stories on one side and gnoseological stories on the other. As in any typological study, I am seeking rather to bring to light the abstract categories that make it possible to account for real differences between one narrative and another. This does not mean, moreover, that a narrative must exhibit one type of transformation to the exclusion of the other. If we go back to "The Swan-Geese," we can find traces of gnoseological organization in it as well. For example, the brother's kidnapping took place in the little girl's absence; in principle, the girl does not know who is responsible, and there would be a place here for a quest for information. But the tale simply says: "The girl guessed that they had taken her brother away," without lingering over this process. On the other hand, Boccaccio's tale rests entirely upon ignorance followed by knowledge. If we want to attach a given narrative to a particular type of narrative organization, we have to look for the qualitative or quantitative predominance of certain transformations, not for their exclusive presence.

A glance at some other examples of gnoseological organization will be helpful. In a work like *La Quête du Graal*,[4] passages recounting actual events are often preceded by passages in which those same events are evoked in the form of a prediction. In this text, such transformations of supposition have a peculiar feature: they all come true, and are even perceived as moral imperatives by the characters. The outcome of the plot is related by Perceval's aunt at the very beginning of the section entitled "Aventures de Perceval": "For it is well known, in this country as elsewhere, that in the end three knights above all others will reap the glory of the Quest: two will be virgins and the third chaste. Of the two virgins, one will be the knight you are looking for, and you will be the other; the third will be Bohort de Gaunes. These three will succeed in the Quest" (118). And there is Perceval's sister, who predicts where her brother and Galahad will die: "For my honor, have me buried in the Spiritual Palace. Do you know why I request this? Because Perceval will be lying there, and you by his side" (272). In a general way, in the whole second part of the text the forthcoming events are first announced by Perceval's sister in the form of imperative predictions.

These suppositions prior to the event are matched by others recalled only after the event has taken place. The chance incidents of his journey lead Galahad to a monastery; the adventure of the shield begins; just as it ends, a heavenly knight appears and declares that everything has been foreseen in advance. "'So here is what you will do,' said Joseph. 'Put the shield where Nasciens is to be buried. To this place Galahad will come, five days after he receives the order of knighthood.' Everything happened as he had said, since on the fifth day you arrived at the abbey where Nasciens's body lies" (82). Gawain has the same experience; immediately after receiving a harsh blow from Galahad's sword, he remembers: "Now it has come true, what I heard the day of Pentecost about the sword I was reaching out for. It was announced to me that before long I would receive a terrible blow, and that is the very sword with which this knight has just struck me. It happened just as it was foretold to me" (230).

But even more characteristic of *La Quête du Graal* than the "announcement" is a transformation, not of supposition, but of knowledge; it consists in a reinterpretation of events that have already taken place. In general, *prud-hommes* and hermits give every earthly action an interpretation in the celestial order, often adding purely terrestrial revelations. Thus when we read the beginning of the story, we think everything is clear: we encounter the noble knights who decide to leave in search of the Holy Grail, and so forth. But little by little the narrative acquaints us with another meaning of these same scenes. Lancelot,

[4] *La Quête du Graal,* ed. Albert Béguin and Yves Bonnefoy (Paris: Editions du Seuil, 1965) 118.

whom we thought strong and perfect, is an incorrigible sinner, living in adultery with Queen Guinevere. Sir Gawain, who was the first to vow to undertake the quest, will never achieve it, for his heart is hard and he does not think enough about God. The knights we first admire are inveterate sinners who will be punished; they have not been to confession for years. When the opening events are alluded to later on, we are in possession of the truth and not deceived by appearances.

The reader's interest is not driven by the question What happens next?, which refers us to the logic of succession or to the mythological narrative. We know perfectly well from the start what will happen, who will reach the Grail, who will be punished and why. Our interest arises from a wholly different question which refers instead to the gnoseological organization: What is the Grail? The Grail narrative relates a quest; what is being sought, however, is not an object but a meaning, the meaning of the word Grail. And since the question has to do with being and not with doing, the exploration of the future is less important than that of the past. Throughout the narrative the reader has to wonder about the meaning of the Grail. The principal narrative is a narrative of knowledge; ideally, it would never end.

The search for knowledge also dominates another type of narrative that we might hesitate to compare to the quest for the Holy Grail: the mystery, or detective story. We know such narratives are constituted by the problematic relation of two stories: the story of the crime, which is missing, and the story of the investigation, which is present, and whose only justification is to acquaint us with the other story. Some element of that first story is indeed made available from the beginning: a crime is committed almost before our eyes; but we have been unable to determine its real agents or motives. The investigation consists in returning over and over to the events, verifying and correcting the smallest details, until the truth about the initial story finally comes out; this is a story of learning. But unlike the Grail story, what characterizes knowledge in detective fiction is that it has only two possible values, true or false. In a detective story, either we know who committed the murder or we do not, whereas the quest for meaning in the Grail story has an infinite number of intermediate degrees, and even in the end the quest's outcome is not certain.

If we take as our third example one of Henry James's tales, we shall see that the gnoseological search can take other forms (Conrad's *Heart of Darkness* presents yet another variant, as we shall see). As in the detective story, James's search focuses on the truth about an actual event, not an abstract entity; but, as in *La Quête du Graal,* at the end of the story we are not sure we possess *the* truth; we have moved, rather, from primary ignorance to a lesser ignorance. *In the Cage,* for example, recounts the experience of a young woman telegraph operator. Her full attention is focused on two people she hardly knows, Captain Everard and Lady Bradeen. She reads the telegrams they send, hears fragments of sentences, but despite her skill at imagining the absent elements, she does not succeed in reconstituting a faithful portrait of the two strangers. Moreover, when she meets the Captain in person it does not help; she can see his physical build, observe his gestures, listen to his voice, but his "essence" remains just as intangible, if not more so, than when the glass cage separated them. The senses retain only appearances; truth is inaccessible.

Comprehension is made particularly difficult by the fact that the telegraph operator pretends to know much more than she really does, when under certain circumstances she has the chance to question intermediary third parties. Thus when she meets a friend, Mrs. Jordan, the friend asks: "'Why, don't you know the scandal? . . . ' Our heroine thought, recollected; . . . 'Oh, there was nothing public . . . '"[5]

James always refuses to name "truth" or "essences" directly; these exist only in the form of multiple appearances. This position has a profound effect on the organization of his works and draws his attention to the techniques of "point of view," which he himself comes to call "that magnificent and masterly indirectness." *In the Cage* gives us the telegraph operator's perception as it bears upon Mrs. Jordan, who herself relates what she has gotten out of her fiancé, Mr. Drake, who in turn has only a remote acquaintance with Captain Everard and Lady Bradeen!

Once again, the process of acquiring information is *dominant* in James's tale, but its presence does not exclude all others. *In the Cage* is also subject to a principle of mythological organization. The original equilibrium of the telegraph operator is disturbed by her encounter with the Captain; at the end of the narrative, however, she returns to her initial project, which was to marry Mr. Mudge. On the other hand, alongside transformations of knowledge as such, there are others that possess the same formal properties without having to do with the same process (the term *gnoseological* no longer applies); this is particularly true of what one might call *subjectivation,* a personal reaction or response to an event. Proust's *A la Recherche du temps perdu* develops this latter transformation to the point of hypertrophy: the most trivial incident of the narrator's life, like the grain of sand around which a pearl grows, serves as a pretext for long descriptions on the way the event is experienced by one character or another.

Here we need to distinguish two ways of judging transformation: according to their *formative* power or to their *evocative* power. By formative power I mean the transformation's aptitude for forming a narrative sequence all by itself. It is difficult (although not impossible) to imagine a narrative that would include only transformations of subjectivization, a narrative that would be reduced, in other words, to the description of an event and various characters' reactions to it. Even Proust's novel includes elements of mythological narrative: the narrator's inability to write will be overcome; Swann's way and Guermantes' way, at first completely separate, will converge with Gilberte's marriage to Saint-Loup. Negation is clearly a transformation with great formative power; but the coupling of ignorance (or error) and knowledge also serves quite often to frame narratives. The other devices of the mythological

[5] Henry James, *In the Cage* (New York: Fox Duffield Company, 1906).

narrative seem less apt (at least in our culture) to form sequences on their own. A narrative that included only modal sequences would resemble a didactic and moralizing text, with sequences like the following: "*X* must behave like a good Christian – *X* behaves like a good Christian." A narrative formed exclusively of transformations of intention would resemble certain passages in *Robinson Crusoe:* Robinson decides to build himself a house – he builds himself a house: Robinson decides to put a fence around his garden – he puts a fence around his garden; and so on.

But this formative (or syntactic) power of certain transformations must not be confused with what we particularly appreciate in a narrative, either what is richest in meaning or what makes it possible to distinguish one narrative from another. I recall that one of the most exciting scenes of a spy movie, *The Ipcress File,* consisted in showing us the main character in the process of fixing himself an omelet. Naturally, the narrative importance of that episode was nonexistent (he could just as well have eaten a ham sandwich); but this crucial scene became something like the emblem of the film as a whole. This is what I call the evocative power of an action; it seems to me that transformations of manner in particular serve to characterize a given fictional universe as opposed to some other, yet on their own they would have great difficulty producing an autonomous narrative sequence.

Now that we are beginning to become familiar with this opposition between the principle of succession and the principle of transformation (and with the variants of the transformation principle), we may wonder whether it is not identical to Jakobson's opposition between metonymy and metaphor. The association is possible, but I do not think it necessary. It is difficult to assimilate all transformations to relations of similarity, just as it is difficult to assimilate all similarity to metaphor. Nor does the principle of succession have anything to gain by being called metonymy, or contiguity, especially since the former is essentially temporal and the latter spatial. The association would be all the more problematic in that, according to Jakobson, "the principle of similarity underlies poetry," and that "prose, on the contrary, is forwarded essentially by contiguity,"[6] whereas from our viewpoint succession and transformation are equally necessary to narrative. If we had to contrast narrative and poetry (or epic and lyric), we might focus, in the first place, on the transitive or intransitive character of the sign (in this we are in agreement with Jakobson); in the second place, on the nature of the temporality represented: discontinuous in one instance, a perpetual presence in the other (which does not mean atemporality); in the third place, on the nature of the names that occupy the place of the semantic subject, or theme, in the one case and the other: narrative recognizes only individual names in the position of subject, whereas poetry allows both individual names and common nouns. Philosophical discourse,

[6] Roman Jakobson, "Two Aspects of Language and Two Types of Aphasic Disturbance," in *Selected Writings II: Word and Language* (The Hague: Mouton, 1971) 258–9.

for its part, is characterized both by the exclusion of individual names and by atemporality; in this view poetry is an intermediate form between narrative discourse and philosophical discourse.

But let us return to narrative and ask rather whether all relations between one action and others can be distributed between the mythological and the gnoseological types. The tale Propp analyzed included an episode that I skimmed over earlier. Having set out to find her brother, the little girl encountered some potential donors. First she met a stove whom she asked for information and who promised it to her if she would eat one of its rye-cakes; she insolently refused. Then she met an apple tree and a river: "similar proposals and similar arrogant replies."[7]

Precisely how are these three episodes related? We have seen that, in relations of transformation, two propositions turn out to be associated; the transformation involves a modification of the predicate. But at present, in the three actions Propp describes, the predicate specifically remains unchanged: in each instance, one character offers, the other insolently refuses. What changes are the agents (the subjects) of each proposition, or the circumstances. Rather than being transformations of each other, these propositions appear as *variants* of a single situation, or as parallel applications of the same rule.

One might then conceive of a third type of narrative organization, no longer mythological or gnoseological but, let us say, *ideological*, inasmuch as an abstract rule, an idea, produces the various peripeties. The relation of the propositions among themselves is no longer direct; one no longer moves from a negative to a positive version, or from ignorance to knowledge. Instead, actions are linked through the intermediary of an abstract formula: in the case of "The Swan-Geese," that of the proffered assistance and the insolent refusal. Often, in order to find the relation between two actions that are completely independent of each other in material terms, we must look for a highly developed abstraction. I have attempted to describe the logical rules, the ideological imperatives that govern the events of the narrative universe of a number of different texts (this could also be done for each of the narratives we have referred to above). Thus, in *Les Liaisons dangereuses,* all the characters' actions can be presented as the product of some very simple and abstract rules; these rules in turn refer to the organizing ideology of the work as a whole.

The same is true for Constant's *Adolphe.* The rules that govern the characters' behavior can be reduced to two. The first stems from the logic of desire as asserted by this text, which might be formulated as follows: one desires what one does not have, one flees what one has. Consequently, obstacles reinforce desire, and any help weakens it. A first blow strikes Adolphe's love when Ellénore leaves Count P . . . to come live with Adolphe. A second blow is struck when she devotes herself to caring for Adolphe after he is wounded. Each of Ellénore's sacrifices exasperates Adolphe: they leave him fewer and fewer things to desire. On the other hand, when Adolphe's father decides to

[7] Propp, *Morphology of the Folktale,* 88.

bring about the separation of the couple, the opposite effect is achieved, and Adolphe states this explicitly: "Thinking you are separating me from her, you may well attach me to her for ever."[8] The tragic aspect of the situation stems from the fact that desire, in order to follow this particular logic, still does not stop being desire, that is, does not stop causing unhappiness in the one who is unable to satisfy it.

The second law of this universe, also a moral law, is formulated by Constant as follows: "The great question in life is the pain one causes and the most ingenious metaphysics cannot justify a man who has broken the heart which loves him" (169). One cannot govern one's life by the search for good, for one person's happiness is always another's misfortune. But one can organize one's life on the basis of the requirement that one should do as little harm as possible: this negative value turns out to be the only one to have the status of an absolute here. The commandments of this second law take precedence over those of the first when the two are in contradiction. This is why Adolphe has so much trouble telling Ellénore the "truth." "Whilst speaking thus, I saw her face suddenly bathed in tears. I stopped, I retraced my steps, I retracted and explained" (89). In chapter 6, Ellénore hears him out; she falls into a faint, and Adolphe can only assure her of his love. In chapter 8, he has a pretext for leaving her but fails to exploit it: "Could I punish her for an imprudence which I made her commit and, with cold hypocrisy, find a pretext in these imprudences to abandon her without pity?" (139). Pity takes precedence over desire.

Thus isolated and independent actions, often accomplished by different characters, reveal the same abstract logic, the same ideological organization.

Ideological organization seems to possess a weak formative power: narratives that do not frame the actions that result from this organization with another order, adding a second organization to the first, are hard to find. For one can illustrate a logic or an ideology ad infinitum; and there is no reason for one particular illustration to precede – or follow – any other. Thus in *Les Liaisons dangereuses* the actions described are presented within a framework based on ideological organization: the exceptional state constituted by the reign of the "roués," Valmont and Merteuil, will be replaced by a return to traditional morality.

The cases of *Adolphe* and Dostoevsky's *Notes from the Underground,* another text illustrative of ideological organization, are a little different, as we shall see in detail in a later chapter. Another order – which is not the simple absence of the preceding ones – is instituted. It consists of relations that might be called "spatial": repetitions, antitheses, and gradations. Thus in *Adolphe,* the sequence of chapters follows a precise route: there is a portrait of Adolphe in chapter one; we observe the development of his sentiments in chapters two and three, their slow disintegration in chapters four through ten. Each new manifestation of Adolphe's feelings has to be superior to the previous one in the rising section,

---

[8] Benjamin Constant, *Adolphe, and the Red Note-Book,* intro. Harold Nicolson, trans. Carl Wildman (Indianapolis: Bobbs-Merrill, 1959) 104.

inferior in the descending section. The end becomes possible owing to an event that seems to have an exceptional narrative status: death. In *Notes from the Underground,* the succession of events is determined both by gradation and by the law of contrast. The scene with the officer presents in summary form the two roles available to the narrator; next he is humiliated by Zverkov, and he humiliates Lisa in turn, even more seriously. The narrative is interrupted owing to the announcement of a different ideology, embodied by Lisa, which consists in rejecting the master–slave logic and in loving others for themselves.

Once again, it is clear that individual narratives exemplify more than one type of narrative organization (in fact, any one of them could have served to illustrate all of these organizational principles); but the analysis of a specific type is more helpful for the comprehension of a particular text.

One might make an analogous observation by radically changing levels and declaring that a narrative analysis will be more helpful for the study of certain types of texts than for others. For what I am examining here is not *text,* which has its own varieties, but *narrative,* which may play an important role or none at all in the structure of a text, and which appears in literary texts as well as in other symbolic systems. It is a given that the narratives that all society seems to need in order to live depend today, not on literature, but on cinema: filmmakers tell us stories, whereas writers play with words. The typological remarks I have just presented thus have to do in principle not only with literary narratives, such as the ones I used as examples, but with all types of narrative; they stem less from *poetics* than from a discipline that seems to me to have every right to exist and that should be called *narratology.*

4 Reading as Construction

What is everywhere passes unnoticed. Nothing is more commonplace than the experience of reading, and nothing is less well known. Reading is taken for granted to such an extent that at first glance it seems nothing need be said about it.

In literary studies the problem of reading has occasionally (although rarely) been taken up, from two very different points of view. The first approach takes readers into account, in their historical, social, collective, or individual diversity. The second reckons with the image of the reader as represented in certain texts: the reader as character or "narratee." But there is one area, the logic of reading, that remains unexplored. This logic is not represented in texts, yet it antedates individual difference.

Of the various types of reading, I shall be concerned here with only one, though hardly the least important: the reading of classic texts of fiction, or more precisely texts said to be representational. This is the only type of reading undertaken in the mode of construction.

Even though we no longer look at art and literature as imitation, it is difficult to give up a way of seeing inscribed in our linguistic habits that leads us to conceive of the novel in terms of representation, transposition of a preexisting reality. Even if this view aims to characterize merely the process of creation, it already poses a problem; it is unequivocally distorting inasmuch as it deals with the text itself. What exists, first of all, is the text, and nothing else; it is only by subjecting the text to a particular type of reading that we construct an imaginary universe on the basis of the text. The novel does not imitate reality, it creates reality. This pre-Romantic formula is not simply a terminological innovation; only the perspective of construction allows us to understand correctly the way a so-called representational text functions.

The question of reading can thus be recast in narrower terms. How does a text lead us to the construction of an imaginary universe? What aspects of the text determine the construction we produce when we read, and in what way?

Let us begin with what is simplest.

Referential Discourse

Only referential sentences permit construction; however, not every sentence is necessarily referential. This is a fact well known to linguists and logicians; we need not linger over it.

Comprehension is a different process from construction. Let us take two sentences from *Adolphe*: "I felt she was better than I; I despised myself for not being worthy of her. It is a fearful misfortune not to be loved when you love; but it is a much greater misfortune to be loved passionately when you love no longer."[1] The first sentence is referential; it evokes an event (Adolphe's feelings). The second, a maxim, is nonreferential. The difference between the two is signaled by grammatical indices: the maxim requires the present tense, it requires the third person, and it includes no anaphors.

A sentence is either referential or not; there is no intermediate degree. However, the words that make it up are not all alike in this respect; the author's lexical choices produce widely differing results. Two independent oppositions seem particularly relevant here: the opposition between what is perceptible and what is not, and the opposition between the particular and the general. For instance, Adolphe refers to his past as "a dissipated life" (47). The expression evokes perceptible events, but at an extremely general level; we can readily imagine thousands of pages that would describe exactly the same phenomenon. However, in another sentence, "I found in my father not a censor but a cold and caustic observer, who would first smile with pity, and who would soon end the conversation with impatience" (47), perceptible and nonperceptible events are juxtaposed. The father's smile and his silence are observable phenomena, while his pity and his impatience are suppositions – no doubt justified – about feelings to which we have no direct access.

A given text of fiction typically offers examples of all these registers of discourse (although their distribution varies according to periods and schools, or as a function of the global organization of the text). The nonreferential sentences are not retained in the course of a reading as construction; they call for a different reading. The referential sentences lead to constructions of varying nature, depending on whether they are more or less general, whether they evoke more or less perceptible events.

Narrative Filters

The qualities of discourse mentioned so far may be identified apart from any context: they are inherent in the sentences themselves. However, we read entire texts, not just sentences. Thus we compare sentences among themselves from the viewpoint of the imaginary universe they help construct; and we discover that they differ in several ways, or according to several parameters. Narrative analysts seem to have agreed on three parameters: mood, time, and point of view. Here again, we are on relatively well-known territory

---

[1] Benjamin Constant, *Adolphe, and the Red Note-Book,* intro. Harold Nicolson, trans. Carl Wildman (Indianapolis: Bobbs-Merrill, 1959) 99.

(I have attempted to establish its highlights in my *Introduction to Poetics*[2]); we must simply consider it now from the viewpoint of reading.

Mood. Direct discourse is the only way to eliminate all difference between narrative discourse and the universe it evokes: as the words used are exactly the same, construction is direct and immediate. This is not the case for non-verbal events or for transposed discourse. Let us consider the following statement from *Adolphe*: "Our host, who had chatted with a Neapolitan who served this man without knowing his name, told me that this person was not travelling out of curiosity, for he visited no ruins, nor historic sites, nor monuments, nor men" (45). We can imagine the narrator's conversation with the host, although it is improbable that the latter, even in Italian, used a sentence identical to the one introduced by the phrase "told me that." The construction of the conversation between host and servant, which is also evoked, is much less determined; we enjoy correspondingly greater freedom if we wish to construct it in detail. Finally, the conversations and other shared activities of Adolphe and the servant are entirely undetermined; only a global impression is transmitted.

The discourse of a narrator may likewise be considered an example of direct style, although raised to the next highest degree, especially if (as for example in the case of *Adolphe*) the narrator is represented in the text. The maxim, earlier excluded from reading as construction, is recuperated here, no longer as utterance but as enunciation. The fact that Adolphe the narrator has formulated such a maxim regarding the misfortune of being loved provides information about his character, and thus about the imaginary universe to which he belongs.

Temporality. In the imaginary universe, time (historical time) is ordered chronologically. However, the sentences of the text do not, cannot, obey that order; the reader thus proceeds unconsciously with the task of reordering. Similarly, certain sentences evoke several distinct but comparable events (the iterative narrative); in the course of construction, we reestablish plurality.

Point of view. The "view" we have of the events evoked obviously determines the way we go about the task of construction. For example, in the case of a valorizing point of view, we allow for (a) the event related, and (b) the attitude of whoever "sees" with respect to that event. We can also distinguish information that a sentence provides about its object from information concerning its subject; thus *Adolphe*'s "editor" can consider only the second type, as he comments on the narrative we have just read: "I hate the vanity which is only concerned with itself when recounting the evil it has done, which seeks to inspire pity in describing itself and which, being indestructible, hovers over the ruins only to analyse itself instead of to repent" (169–70). The editor thus constructs the subject of the narrative (Adolphe the narrator) and not its object (Adolphe the character and Ellénore).

[2] Tzvetan Todorov, *Introduction to Poetics,* intro. Peter Brooks, trans. Richard Howard (Minneapolis: University of Minnesota Press, 1981).

Readers typically fail to realize to what extent the fictional text is repetitive, or, as the case may be, redundant; we may suggest with confidence that every event in the story is related at least twice. These repetitions are modulated, most often, by the filters we have just listed: a conversation is reproduced on one occasion, summarily evoked on another; an event is observed from several viewpoints; it is evoked in the future, in the present, and in the past. Moreover, any one of these parameters may be combined with any of the others.

Repetition plays a major role in the process of construction, since from *several* narratives the reader has to construct a *single* event. The relationships among repetitive narratives vary from identity to contradiction; and even material identity does not necessarily lead to identity of meaning (Coppola's film *The Conversation* provides a good example). The functions of these repetitions are just as diverse: they help establish the facts (in the detective story) or help undermine them: thus, in *Adolphe,* the fact that within a very short span of time a single character can have contradictory views of a single phenomenon leads us to understand that psychic states do not exist in isolation, but always with respect to an interlocutor, a partner. Benjamin Constant himself formulates the law of this universe as follows: "The object that escapes us is necessarily entirely different from the one that pursues us."[3]

If we are to be able to construct an imaginary universe upon reading a text, then the text must first of all be referential in itself; at this point, having read it, we allow our imagination to "work" by filtering the information received according to questions of the following types: To what extent is the description of that universe accurate? In what order did the events occur (time)? To what extent must we take into account distortions that can be attributed to the "reflector" of the narrative (point of view)? But all this allows us only to begin the task of reading.

Signification and Symbolization

How do we know what happens when we read? Through introspection; and if we seek to confirm an impression, we can fall back upon accounts that others may offer us of their reading. However, two accounts dealing with the same text will never be identical. How can we explain this diversity? By the fact that these accounts describe not the universe of the book itself but that universe transformed, as it is found in the psyche of each individual. The stages of this itinerary may be schematized as follows:

1. The author's narrative		4. The reader's narrative
↓		↑
2. Imaginary universe evoked by the author	→	3. Imaginary universe constructed by the reader

We may wonder whether the difference between stages 2 and 3, illustrated in our schema, actually exists. Are there any constructions other than individual

---

[3] Constant, "Journal," in *Oeuvres* (Paris: Gallimard [Editions de la Pléiade], 1957) 302.

ones? It is easy to show that the answer to that question must be in the affirmative. No reader of *Adolphe* can doubt that Ellénore lives first with Count P . . . , that she then leaves him and lives with Adolphe, that they separate, that she rejoins Adolphe in Paris, and so on. On the other hand, there is no way to establish with the same degree of certainty whether Adolphe is weak or simply sincere.

The reason for this duality is that the text evokes phenomena according to two different modes that I propose to call signification and symbolization. Ellénore's trip to Paris is *signified* by the words of the text. Adolphe's (possible) weakness is *symbolized* by other phenomena of the imaginary universe, which for their part are signified by words. For example, the fact that Adolphe is unable to defend Ellénore in his discourse is signified; in turn, this fact symbolizes his inability to love. The signified facts are *understood*; for this level of understanding, the reader need only know the language in which the text is written. The symbolized facts are *interpreted*; and the interpretations vary from one subject to another.

The relation between stages 2 and 3, indicated above, is thus a relation of symbolization (whereas the relation between 1 and 2, or 3 and 4, is one of signification). Moreover, we are not dealing with a unique relation, but with a heterogenous set of relations. In the first place, we are foreshortening: 4 is (almost) always shorter than 1, thus 3 is also poorer than 2. In the second place, we are mistaken. In both cases, the study of the passage from stage 2 to stage 3 leads us to projective psychology. The transformations that are brought about inform us as to the subject of the reading: why does that reader retain (or even add) certain facts rather than certain others? But other transformations exist that inform us about the process of reading itself, and these will be our chief concern here.

It is difficult for me to say whether the state of affairs I observe in the most varied examples from fiction is a universal phenomenon or whether it is historically and culturally conditioned. The fact remains that, in all the examples, symbolization and interpretation (the passage from stage 2 to stage 3) imply the existence of some *determinism* of the phenomena in question. Perhaps the reading of other texts, for example lyric poems, imposes a task of symbolization that depends upon other presuppositions (universal analogy)? I do not know. It is nevertheless the case that, in a fictional text, symbolization depends upon the explicit or implicit recognition of a principle of causality. Thus the questions one raises about the events that constitute the mental image of stage 2 are of the following order: What is the cause of these events? What is their effect? The answers will be added to the mental image as we find it in stage 3.

Let us acknowledge that this determinism is universal; what is assuredly not universal is the form it takes on in a particular case. The simplest form, though one that is not widespread in our culture as a *norm* of reading, consists in the construction of another fact of the same nature. A reader may say to herself: if John killed Peter (a fact that is present in the fiction), it is because Peter was sleeping with John's wife (a fact absent from the fiction). This reasoning, typical of juridical investigations, is not applied seriously to novels: we tacitly acknowledge that the author does not cheat and that he has transmitted to us (has signified) all the events that are relevant for the comprehension of the story (the case of *Armance* is exceptional). Similarly for the consequences: many books exist that are sequels to other books, which spell out the consequences of the imaginary universe represented by the first text; but the content of the second book is not usually considered as being *inherent* in the universe of the first one. Once again, the practices of reading are different from those of everyday life.

We normally proceed according to a different causality when we are engaged in a construction-reading; the causes and consequences of the event are to be sought in a matter that is not homogeneous to it. Two cases seem to be the most common (as Aristotle also remarked): the event is perceived as the consequence (and/or the cause) either of a character trait or of an impersonal law. *Adolphe* contains numerous examples of both interpretations, integrated into the text itself. Here is how Adolphe describes his father: "I do not remember in my first eighteen years ever having had an hour's conversation with him . . . I did not then know what timidity meant . . ." (48). The first sentence signifies a fact (the absence of prolonged conversation). The second brings us to consider this fact as symbolizing a character trait, which is shyness: if Adolphe's father behaves this way, it is because he is shy. The character trait is the cause of the action. And here is an example of the second case: "I told myself I should not be over-hasty as Ellénore was not prepared for the confession I was contemplating, and it would be better to wait longer. In order to live at peace with ourselves, we almost always disguise impotence or weakness as calculated actions and systems, and so we satisfy that part of us which is observing the other" (63–4). Here the first sentence describes the event, and the second gives the reason for it, which is a universal law of human behavior, not an individual character trait. It is this second type of causality that is dominant in *Adolphe,* we might add: this novel illustrates psychological *laws,* not individual psychologies.

After constructing the events that make up a story, we then give ourselves over to the task of reinterpretation, which allows us to construct the work's characters on the one hand, the system of ideas and values underlying the text on the other. This reinterpretation is not arbitrary; it is controlled by two series of constraints. The first is implicit in the text itself: it suffices for the author to spend a little time teaching us how to interpret the events he evokes. This is the case of the excerpts from *Adolphe* that I have just cited: after establishing some determinist explanations, Constant need not always spell out the cause of an event; we have learned the lesson, and we shall continue to interpret as he has taught us to do. Such an interpretation, present in the text of the book, thus has a double function: on the one hand, it teaches us the cause of a particular fact (exegetic function); on the other hand, it initiates us into the interpretive system that will be the author's throughout the book (metaexegetic function). The second series of constraints comes from the cultural context: if we read that so-and-so has cut his wife into little pieces, we do not need any textual indications to tell us that so-and-so is a cruel man. These cultural constraints, which are nothing but the commonplaces of a social group (notions its members deem plausible), are modified over time, which makes it possible to explain the different ways earlier texts have been interpreted. For example, as extramarital love is no longer considered proof of a corrupt soul, we sometimes have trouble understanding the condemnations leveled upon so many fictional heroines of the past.

Characters, ideas: entities of this sort are symbolized through actions, but they may also be signified. This is precisely the case in the excerpts from *Adolphe* cited above: an action symbolized the father's shyness, but then Adolphe signified it for us when he said "my father was timid" (48). The same thing happened with the general maxim. The characters and ideas can thus be evoked in two ways, directly or indirectly. Bits of information drawn from each source will be confronted by the reader during the process of construction; they may or may not be compatible. The relative dosage of these two types of information has varied considerably, it goes without saying, in the course of literary history; Hemingway does not write like Constant.

The character constituted in this sense has to be distinguished from the cast of "characters": not every "character" in the cast is a character in the first sense. The "character" is a segment of the spatio-temporal universe represented and nothing more; there are characters in this sense as soon as a referential linguistic form (proper names, certain nominal syntagmas, personal pronouns) appears in the text with regard to an anthropomorphic being. As such, the "character" has no content: someone is identified without being described. We may imagine texts – and they exist – in which the "characters" are no more than this: they are the agents of a series of actions. But as soon as psychological determinism surfaces, the "character" is transformed into a character: he acts in a given way *because* he is timid, weak, courageous, and so forth. Without determinism (of this sort), there are no characters.

The construction of the character is a compromise between difference and repetition. On the one hand, continuity must be assured: the reader has to construct the *same* character. This continuity is already given by the identity of the name; indeed, this is the name's main function. From this point on, all sorts of blends are possible: all the actions may illustrate the same character trait, or the "character" may behave in contradictory ways, or he may change the circumstantial aspects of his life, or he may undergo a profound character modification. Examples come readily to mind; we need not recall them here. Once again, the choices are dictated by the history of styles rather than by authorial idiosyncrasy.

Character, then, may be an effect of reading; there exists a psychologizing reading to which any text may be submitted. But in reality it is not an arbitrary effect; it is no accident that we find characters in eighteenth- and nineteenth-century novels, and that we do not find them either in Greek tragedies or in folktales. The text itself always contains an indication of the way it is to be read.

Construction as Theme

One of the difficulties of studying reading stems from the fact that reading is hard to observe: introspection is uncertain, and psychosocial investigation is tedious. So it is with some relief that we discover the work of construction represented within fictional texts themselves – where it is much easier to study.

The fictional text takes construction as a theme simply because it is impossible to evoke human life without mentioning this essential process. Each "character" is obliged, on the basis of information she receives, to construct the facts and the "characters" that surround her. In this she is rigorously parallel to the reader who constructs the imaginary universe on the basis of his own information (the text, the plausible); reading thus (inevitably) becomes one of the themes of the book.

However, this thematics may be more or less valorized, more or less exploited. In *Adolphe,* for example, it is exploited in a very partial fashion: only the ethical undecidability of the actions is put on display. If we wish to use fictional texts as material for the study of construction, we have to choose those in which it becomes one of the major themes. Stendhal's *Armance* is one such example.

The entire intrigue of this novel, indeed, is governed by the quest for knowledge (gnoseological narrative). An erroneous construction on Octave's part serves as a point of departure: on the evidence of specific behavior, Octave believes that Armance values money too highly (interpretation proceeding from the action to the character trait); no sooner is this misunderstanding dissipated than it is followed by another one, its symmetrical opposite: Armance now believes that Octave values money too highly. This initial game of hide-and-seek institutes the figure of constructions to come. Armance then correctly constructs her feeling for Octave; but it takes Octave ten chapters to discover that what he feels for Armance is not called *friendship* but *love.* During five chapters, Armance believes that Octave does not love her; Octave believes that Armance does not love him during the fifteen middle chapters of the book; the same misunderstanding is repeated at the end. The "characters" spend their lives searching for truth, that is, constructing the events and facts that surround them. The tragic ending of the love relation is not due, as has often been suggested, to impotence, but to a lack of knowledge. Octave commits suicide owing to a faulty construction: he believes that Armance no longer loves him. As Stendhal declared in an emblematic sentence: "Penetration, not character, was what he lacked."[4]

From this rapid summary we can already see that several aspects of the

---

[4] Stendhal, *Armance,* trans. Gilbert and Suzanne Sale (London: The Merlin Press, 1960) 64.

process of construction may vary. One may be the agent or the client, the sender or the receiver of information; one may also be both. Octave is the agent when he conceals or reveals; the client when he learns or misjudges. One may construct a fact (in the "first degree") or someone else's construction of that fact (in the second degree). Thus Armance gives up her marriage to Octave because she imagines what others would imagine in that case. "In the eyes of the world I should be a lady companion who has seduced the son of the house. Even now I can hear the comments of Mme la Duchesse d'Ancre, and even of the most respectable women, such as the Marquise de Seyssins, who sees in Octave a husband for one of her daughters" (91). Similarly, Octave gives up suicide by constructing the possible constructions of others. "If I take my life, Armance will be compromised; the whole of society will spend a week inquisitively prying into the minutest details of this evening, and every one of those gentlemen who were present will feel sanctioned to tell a different tale" (114).

What we learn in *Armance* in particular is that construction may succeed or fail; and if all successes are alike (that is the "truth"), the failures vary, as do their causes: deficiencies in the information transmitted. The simplest case is that of total ignorance: up to a certain point in the intrigue, Octave conceals the very existence of a secret involving himself (active role), while Armance also is ignorant of the existence of that secret (passive role). Then the existence of the secret may be known, but without any additional information (Armance supposes that Octave has assassinated someone). Illusion constitutes a still higher degree: the agent does not conceal but disguises; the dupe is not ignorant but is misled. That is the most frequent case in the book: Armance disguises her love for Octave by claiming that she will marry someone else; Octave thinks that Armance looks on him only as a friend. One may be both agent and dupe of disguise: thus Octave hides from himself the fact that he loves Armance. Finally, the agent may reveal the truth and the dupe may learn it.

Ignorance, imagination, illusion, truth: the process of acquiring knowledge passes through three stages at least before leading the character to a definitive construction. The same stages are clearly possible in the reading process. Normally the construction represented in the text is isomorphic to the one that takes the text itself as the point of departure. What the characters do not know, the reader does not know either. To be sure, the other combinations are also possible. In the detective story, it is the Watson character who constructs as the reader does, but the Sherlock Holmes character constructs better: the two roles are both necessary.

The Other Readings

The failures of construction-reading in no way threaten its identity: we do not cease to construct because the information is insufficient or erroneous. Such failures, on the contrary, only intensify the process of construction. It is nevertheless possible that construction may cease to be produced, and that other types of reading may come to take its place.

The differences between one reading and another do not necessarily turn up where one would expect to find them. For example, there does not seem to be a great gap between construction on the basis of a literary text and construction on the basis of some other text that is referential but not literary. This proximity was understood in the proposition stated in the preceding paragraph, namely, that the construction of characters (on the basis of non-literary materials) was analogous to that of the reader (on the basis of the text of a novel). One does not construct "fiction" differently from "reality." The historian who studies written documents or the judge who depends upon oral testimony both reconstitute the "facts," and their procedures are in principle no different from those of the reader of *Armance*; which does not mean there are no differences in detail.

A more difficult question, and one that goes beyond the framework of this study, concerns the relation between construction on the basis of verbal information and construction on the basis of other perceptions. After smelling a leg of lamb, we construct a leg of lamb; similarly, upon hearing something, we construct a view of it, and so on; that is what Piaget called the *construction of the real*. The differences are likely to be greater here.

But it is not necessary to go so far from the novel to find the material that forces us to undertake another type of reading. There are indeed literary texts that lead to no construction at all; these are nonrepresentational texts. Several cases need to be distinguished even here. The most obvious one is that of a kind of poetry, usually called lyrical, which does not describe events, which evokes nothing that is external to itself. The modern novel, in turn, obliges us to undertake a different reading: the text is indeed referential, but construction does not occur, for it is in some sense undecidable. This effect is achieved by the disruption of one or another of the mechanisms necessary to construction, as they have been described in the foregoing paragraphs. To take just one example: we have seen that the identity of the character was grounded on the identity and unambiguousness of his name. Let us now imagine that, in a text, the same character is mentioned in turn by different names: at one point he is called "John," at another point "Peter," or he is referred to as "the man with black hair" and then as "the man with blue eyes," without anything indicating that those two expressions refer to the same individual; or let us imagine that "John" designates not just one but three or four characters. In each case the result will be the same: construction will no longer be possible, for the text will be representatively undecidable. We can see how this is different from the failures of construction mentioned earlier: we have moved from the unknown or ill-known to the unknowable. This modern literary practice has an extraliterary counterpart: schizophrenic discourse. Even as it maintains its representational intention, schizophrenic discourse makes construction impossible, through a series of devices it appropriates.

For the time being, let us be satisfied to have marked the place of these other readings alongside reading as construction. Recognition of this latter sort of reading is all the more necessary in that the individual reader, oblivious to the theoretical refinements he is exemplifying, reads the same text in several different ways at once, or one after the other. His activity is so natural to him that it remains imperceptible. Thus we have to learn to construct reading – whether as construction or as deconstruction.

5 A Poetic Novel

At three points in his novel *Henry von Ofterdingen,* Novalis contrasts two types of men.[1] The first time, the contrasting is done by the protagonist Henry himself, during a conversation with the merchants who accompany him on his travels. The opposition is presented, more specifically, in terms of "two roads leading to the knowledge of human history. The one, wearisome and without visible goal, with countless twists and turns – the way of experience: the other, hardly more than a single leap – the way of intuition. He who takes the first road has to figure out one thing from another by laborious calculation, while he who takes the second immediately penetrates to the essence of every event and object and is able to contemplate these essences in their vital complex interrelationship and easily compare them with everything else like numbers on a slate" (29–30).

The second opposition is made by the author, at the beginning of chapter 6. Here is his portrait of the first type of men: "People born to carry on trade and business cannot early enough consider and come to grips with everything themselves. . . . They may not yield to the lures of a quiet contemplation. Their soul may not indulge in introspective reverie; it must be steadily directed outward and be an industrious, swiftly-deciding servant of their mind. They are heroes, and around them throng the events that need to be guided and solved. All occurrences turn into history under their influence, and their lives form an unbroken chain of remarkable and splendid, intricate, and strange events" (93).

As for the second type, "it is different with those serene, little-known people whose world is their soul, whose activity is contemplation, whose life is a gradual development of their inner powers. No restlessness exerts an outward drive. A modest possession contents them. The vast drama around them does not tempt them to play a role in it themselves, but it does seem to them

---

[1] Novalis, *Heinrich von Ofterdingen: ein Roman,* in *Novalis Schriften,* ed. Paul Kluckhohn and Richard Samuel (Stuttgart: W. Kohlhammer, 1960) vol. 1, 181–334; *Henry von Ofterdingen: A Novel,* trans. Palmer Hilty (New York: Frederick Ungar, 1974). Passages quoted are from the English translation.

important and marvelous enough to devote their leisure to its contemplation.
. . . Great and complex events would disturb these introverted people. A simple
life is their lot, and only from hearsay and writings may they become acquainted with the rich content and the countless phenomena of the world. . . .
They will never take a step without making the most surprising discoveries
within themselves about the nature and significance of these phenomena.
[These are] the poets . . . " (93–4).

In the third and final instance another character, Klingsohr, sketches in the
same contrast. He limits his remarks to noting the perfect symmetry between
the two types of men: pure heroes, he says, "are the noblest counterpart of
the poets" (114). Making a related comparison, Novalis observes that while
poetry may arouse heroism, heroism never gives rise to poetry.

Let us schematize the opposition as follows, so as to keep it clearly in mind:

Heroes	Poets
experience	contemplation
action	reflection
worldly affairs	essence and meaning of the world
striking and memorable events	existence reduced to utmost simplicity
involvement of the person himself	interest in the world as spectacle
learning spread over time	immediate knowledge
passage from one thing to another by deduction	intuitive grasp of each thing taken separately, then compared
uninterrupted chain of events	increase of inner strengths
maintenance of diversity and singularity	secret identity of things (microcosm and macrocosm)

Now Novalis construes his own novel as belonging to a series which is also
defined in opposition to another. We can see this from some brief remarks
that appear on the drafts and outlines of *Henry von Ofterdingen*.[2] "No historical
transition as such to get to the second part" (341), he writes, and "poetic
ordering and coherence of *Heinrich*" (340). The coherence and continuity are
to be poetic and not historical. The author's friend Tieck offers a more explicit
account of the ordering principle of the novel as Novalis described it to him:[3]
"He had little interest, in fact, in describing a given episode, in taking poetry
[identified as the general subject of the book] in one of its aspects and illustrating
it through stories and characters; on the contrary, as he himself indicated quite
clearly in the last [actually the next-to-last] chapter of the first part, he intended
to express the very essence of poetry and to bring to light its deepest mission.
. . . Nature, history, war or daily life with all its banalities are transformed and

---

[2] Novalis's notes and fragments of drafts for *Heinrich von Ofterdingen* appear in *Novalis Schriften*, Paralipomena, 335–58.
[3] Ludwig Tieck, "Tiecks Bericht über die Fortsetzung," in *Novalis Schriften*, 359–69.

turned into poetry . . . " (369). A historical or narrative genre, evoked indirectly by Tieck as well as Novalis, is contrasted with another genre, which is poetic.

The temptation to link the two oppositions is obvious. Novalis himself does more than hint at such a linkage, not only by calling men "poets" and texts "poetic," but also by concluding the second (and longest) evocation of the two types of men with the statement: "Henry was by nature born to be a poet" (94). *Henry von Ofterdingen,* the story of the life of a poet (and not a hero), embodies both the poetic genre and the poetic man.

Contemporary readers cannot fail to be struck by the discordance between what we see on the title page: *Henry von Ofterdingen: A Novel,* and the tenor of the pages that follow, which can hardly seem novelistic to our eyes. An explanation for this impression can be found, I suggest, in Novalis's own opposition between two types of text: the poetic novel exemplified by *Ofterdingen* on the one hand, and what might be called a narrative novel on the other. And I would be tempted to attribute to these two genres not only the features evoked laconically with respect to texts, but also those features, far more abundant, that characterize the two types of men. The generic features of *Ofterdingen* might even suggest a certain way of characterizing poetic discourse, as it was practiced in the Romantic period and has been practiced since. But how do we move from persons to classes of texts?

Rather than follow Novalis's intuitions, I shall keep them in mind while seeking to make my own explicit. I read the book; I derive from it the impression of a "novel-not-quite-like-other-novels"; and the qualifier "poetic" also comes to mind. Next, I look for the points in the text that have led me to this impression.

Taking myself, then, as an example of the contemporary reader, I try to note all the details that strike me as not particularly "novelistic," right from the start of this "novel." The first action reported (in the second sentence of the text) is that the hero, the adolescent, "thinks": hardly an active action. Moreover, he is not thinking about another concrete action, but about the stories of a stranger, which have to do – and this is all we ever know – with a yearning for a blue flower. Thus instead of an action of the type "The youth does such-and-such," we have "The youth thinks that the stranger said that the blue flower awoke passion"; the action proper comes only in the third degree. The same is true for the second action, which is once again a memory related to stories heard earlier.

In the following episode, the adolescent dreams, and this leads to a dream narrative. Memories and dreams alike displace the narrative onto another level, opening a new narrative line and by that very token suspending the initial story. In this dream, two elements attract my attention. Henry dreams that he is dreaming of "indescribable events" (*Ofterdingen,* 17): a discontinuity that we are beginning to recognize, and that interrupts one of the narratives without being able to express the other. The second element occurs at the end of the dream, and it is truly remarkable only if we forget that we are in a dream: this is the transformation of the blue flower into a "delicate face." If we do not acknowledge the supernatural, we have to look for some allegorical meaning in these words. Might the identity between flower and woman be merely metaphorical?

When the dream is over, we come upon a second action, but one whose character is scarcely more active than the first: the youth (Henry) and his father engage in an abstract discussion of the nature of dreams. Neither its occurrence as an act nor the content of their conversation has any effect whatsoever on the development of the narrative. Dreams are considered as a means of communication; thus there is communication about communication. And other peoples' dreams are evoked without any specification of their content: Henry recounts that the chaplain has recounted a dream.

The father in turn relates memories, which have to do with a meeting with an old man in the course of which a conversation took place on the subject of poetry. Thus the father says that the old man said that the poets said . . . Next he recalls a dream from twenty years before; here on first reading I am struck, as Henry is, by the resemblance between the father's dream and Henry's own. In both, the dreamer goes into a cave in the heart of a mountain, is blinded by light, emerges on the plain and discovers an extraordinary flower. For me, this parallelism further weakens the reality, even the fictional reality, of the actions described – a reality already muddled by the fact that we are dealing with dreams. When I reread the text, I discover new parallels, between another part of this dream and the story's overall development; the same holds true for a part of Henry's earlier dream (the death of the beloved). The chapter ends at the conclusion of this last dream narrative.

To sum up my impression: the primary narrative consists of very little, and that little is continually interrupted by secondary narratives. The primary narrative might be transcribed without too much abridgment as follows: Henry remembers, dreams, wakes up, speaks of dreams in general, listens to his father talk about them. The secondary narratives do not compensate for this brevity (moreover, they themselves are interrupted in turn by third-degree narratives): the actions that constitute them, just like those of the primary narrative, are interior events, first of all, and they entail no consequences whatsoever for the rest of the story. The parallelisms and the allegorical tendencies complete the creation of a very different impression from the one customarily produced by a "novel."

It would be tedious to pursue this reading page by page. Similar devices sustain the "poetic" atmosphere throughout the novel, in my judgment. I shall thus attempt to examine them one by one, taking their other appearances into account. Four types of phenomena attract my attention: the nature of the actions; the narrative embeddings, or the second-degree narratives; the parallelisms; the use of allegory.

1. *Nature of the actions.* The perceptible actions of the first part of *Henry von Ofterdingen* that are not assumed by a secondary narrator can be summarized as follows: Henry leaves on a voyage and arrives at his destination without encountering any obstacle; once there, he falls in love with Mathilda, who

loves him in return. That is all; we may agree that it is not much for 154 pages of text. Not only are Henry's actions few in number, they are not at all extraordinary; they are not "striking and memorable events," as Novalis would say. Quality does not compensate for quantity.

But to arrive at this accounting I observed several constraints. I retained only the perceptible actions, and of those only the ones related directly by the author. In fact, within some of the embedded narratives, we find more perceptible actions: this in the merchants' tales, or in Zulima's speech, the miner's, or the hermit's (we shall set aside for the moment the effect produced by embedding). In the narrative for which the author is directly responsible, there are many other actions; but we might be tempted to call them "reflections" instead, as Novalis suggested. In their own way, these are actions in the second degree, not because they are reported by a second narrator but because they can only take place in reaction to another, necessarily prior action. "Remembering" or "reflecting" or "thinking" are examples: here we are designating Henry's principal activity. His interest in the "spectacle of the world" by far exceeds his own participation in the course of events.

Another activity much valued by the book's characters is talking ("stories and books" occupy a major portion of their time); this is a perceptible action. But we still need to specify the nature of the words spoken and their place within the various conversations. Speaking is, to be sure, a first-degree action, in the sense in which we have just used the term; but then we are taking into account the act of speaking itself, and not what is communicated: for Scheherezade to survive she must speak (well), and what she says hardly matters. Now this aspect of speech is not valorized in Novalis's novel: no special attention is paid to the fact that the characters speak.

However, purely transitive speech is not yet opposed to the novelistic spirit; it suffices to think of that familiar device of the picaresque novel in which the characters string stories together or embed stories within stories. If speech itself is not an action in the strong sense, its content may be a narrative of actions. But, aside from the few exceptions noted, this is not the case for the words exchanged by the characters of *Henry von Ofterdingen*. What they say can be divided into two main categories. On the one hand, they produce poems, spoken or sung. In the third chapter, the future poet is first seized by "an irresistible longing to write a few lines on . . . paper" (41); later, in front of his father-in-law, he gives voice to a song eighty-eight lines long. In the fourth chapter, we first hear the "crusade song," then the "tender, affecting singing of a female voice" (58). In the next chapter, the miner sings twice, the hermit once. In chapter 6, Schwaning sings first, then Klingsohr. In his notes for the second part, Novalis remarked: "An introductory poem, a concluding poem, and titles for each chapter. Between chapters, poetry speaks" (*Schriften*, 341).

In a second frequently encountered type of conversation, the subject is general; this is true of most of the dialogues in *Ofterdingen*. We have already seen that the father and son discuss dreams in general; Henry and the merchants discuss the ways in which history can be known. In another conversation, the same protagonists compare painting, music, and poetry, as do Henry and Klingsohr. In chapter 4, religion is discussed; chapter 5 includes discussions of the riches hidden in the bowels of the earth, and the advantages and disadvantages of solitude. Even the conversation between Henry and Mathilda has more to do with love in general than with the feeling that unites them: more than love "affairs," it is love's "essence" that interests them.

These internal actions (reflection) or abstract actions (discussion) even neutralize the rare moments of action in the strong sense. This is the case with the encounter between Henry and Mathilda, and again with the encounter between the miner and his friends and the hermit. For once we might think we are in a situation worthy of the gothic novel: a nocturnal visit to grottos, the discovery of bones of unknown origin, underground singing. We discover a second cavern, in which a man is seated. Then what happens? The miner and the hermit embark on a highly abstract discussion about the interest of life in society. In another way, the abundant reflections that accompany the slightest action (for example, Henry's departure) play the same neutralizing role.

Hardly "novelistic" in themselves, the actions in *Ofterdingen* produce a similar nonnovelistic effect by the way in which they are strung together. The most powerful systems of causation found at work in a novel are of two types: either one event leads to another (this is the case with the narrative of classical adventures); or else the new action contributes to the discovery of a hidden truth. Neither of these two forms of causality is represented in this book; it holds out no secrets, and the causality of events is limited to sequences of the departure-voyage-arrival variety. An alternative form of causality is that of the psychological novel, in which all the events contribute to the composition of a character (rather the opposite of La Bruyère's *Characters,* in which an individual produces a series of actions illustrating his character). But one cannot say that Henry is a character, and the art of psychological motivation is wholly foreign to Novalis. Nor does this novel display, finally, the causality I have termed "ideological," where all the actions are generated by an abstract law, for example a concept of the moral nature of man, as is the case at roughly the same time for Constant's *Adolphe.*

However, the various events recounted in *Ofterdingen* are not unrelated to each other. Somewhat as in the psychological novel, they all contribute to Henry's development: not the development of his moral character but of his mind. Each successive encounter leads him to discover some aspect of humanity or the world and enriches his inner being. Moreover, we can do no better than to repeat Novalis's own words: Henry's life is a "gradual development of . . . inner powers" (*Ofterdingen,* 93). "Everything he saw and heard seemed merely to push aside new door-bolts in him and to open new windows for him" (94). One of the draft fragments puts it even more forcefully: "In *Henry,* there is finally an exhaustive description of the internal transfiguration of the depths of the soul [*innern Verklärung des Gemüts*]" (*Schriften,* 339). The transformation around which the novel is constructed indeed takes place, but what is transformed is the *Gemüt* alone, and the transformation is carried out entirely through internal events, of which Novalis offers not so much the narrative as the meticulous description.

2. *Embeddings.* The embedding process obviously does not have the same function in Novalis as it does for example in *Don Quixote.* Taking the whole set of embedded passages into account, we may even contend that they are only sporadically narrative. Most of the time, as we have seen, the embedded material consists of songs or abstract reflections. Often, too, Novalis declares that there has been a narrative, but he does not spell out its content: he does this in the first chapter, for instance, with the foreigner's speech and the chaplain's dream. Elsewhere, he settles for statements like these: "Once I heard tell of the days of old" (*Ofterdingen,* 15); "the world was familiar to him only out of stories" (24); "Heinrich's mother . . . began to tell him about . . . the jolly life in Suabia" (26); "the conversation turned to former adventures in war" (54), and so on. Novalis is more concerned with the representation of the enunciation than with the reproduction of the utterance. Let us return to the example of the merchants' first story about a poet. The merchants report that, in the course of their earlier voyages, someone had told them the story of a poet, who was the author of magnificent stories; but the stories themselves, the end point of the triple embedding, are left untold.

As for the few properly narrative embeddings (the merchants' second narrative, the accounts given by Zulima, the miner, or the hermit, and Klingsohr's tale), even if we leave aside everything that distinguishes these narratives as well from traditional stories, we cannot help noting that their distance with respect to the primary narrative makes the reported events less compelling, introduces a supplementary distance between them and the reader.

3. *Parallelism.* The tendency to resemblance or identification governs the relationships among numerous elements of the novel. Tieck summarized this characteristic as follows: "Here are pointed out all the differences through which the epochs seem to distinguish themselves from each other and through which worlds seem to oppose each other with hostility" (*Schriften,* 360). The principal parallelism is that of the two parts; since the second part was never written, we must again let Tieck explain: "This second part is entitled 'Accomplishment,' just as the first had been given the title 'Waiting,' because the reader was supposed to see the unfolding and accomplishment of all that, in the other part, could be guessed and foretold" (359). Henry would thus have "lived again, but on a new and much ampler plane than in the first part: his experience of nature, of life and death, of war, the Orient, history and poetry" (366–7).

This general parallelism is multiplied in numerous ways. We have seen the resemblance between the father's dream and the son's; Tieck also reveals that, at the beginning of the second part, "the gardener with whom Henry converses is the same man who had earlier welcomed Henry's father" (360). When he meets Mathilda, Henry says: "Do I not feel as I did in that dream when I saw

the blue flower?" (*Ofterdingen*, 104). Novalis takes the characters' mutual identification to great lengths; he includes the following notes in an outline destined
for the second part: "Klingsohr is the monarch of Atlantis. Heinrich's mother
is Imagination; his father, Meaning. Schwaning is the Moon, and the antique
collector is the Miner and also Iron. . . . The emperor Friedrich is Arcturus"
(*Schriften*, 342). Mathilda is also Cyané, and at the same time Zulima (and also
Poetry, and the blue flower, and Edda); and Novalis writes: "The girl is triune [*dreieiniges Mädchen*]" (342). Novalis would call these all "tableau figures,"
inviting us to compare them and even to consider them mutually
interchangeable.

When an embedded narrative resembles the embedding narrative, so that
the part resembles the whole, or, as Novalis might say, when we encounter
"a small-scale image of the larger world," we are dealing with what is now
called *the abyss narrative*. A striking feature of *Ofterdingen* is the abundance of
such images. They are of two types: some have to do with art or poetry in
general (the code); others, with the particular book (the message). There is
nothing astonishing about the former: Tieck reported Novalis's intention to
write other novels in order to treat different subjects, "just as he had treated
poetry in *Ofterdingen*" (359); the book's main character is in fact a poet. The
merchants, the hermit, Henry, and especially Klingsohr make quite elaborate
statements about poetry; moreover, we have seen that the subject is really no
different, even when the topic of discussion is types of men. The embedding
device of the novel itself is also repeated on numerous occasions; we saw at
least a partial example in the opening dreams. The fusions of characters provide
other examples: the tale that fills the third chapter is a reduced image of the
whole, since Klingsohr is the king of Atlantis and Henry is the poet who
marries his daughter. The draft fragments that deal with the book announce
other, unrealized reflections: "the story of the *novel* itself" (340); "she tells
Henry his own story" (343).

But the most thorough-going and spectacular *mise en abîme* is that of the
fifth chapter, where Henry discovers his own story in a book belonging to the
hermit. He does not understand the language in which the book is written,
to be sure, but he can figure out the story from the illustrations; the resemblance
is clear, a "complete similarity" (*Ofterdingen*, 91). He even discovers in one
picture "the cave, the hermit, and the miner at his side" (91); he almost sees
himself looking at the picture that shows him looking at the picture, and so
on. The only difference is a temporal one: "their clothes were altered and
appeared to be those of another age" (91). The hermit adds that "it is a novel
about the wondrous fortunes of a poet, in which poesy is presented and praised
in its manifold relations" (91). The parallel becomes truly striking when,
knowing as we do the fate reserved for *Henry von Ofterdingen*, we learn that
"the conclusion is missing in this manuscript" (91).

Alongside these repetitions and doublings that the reader discovers, there
are others of a different sort that simply concern the way the characters perceive
the world around them. Their lives are full of presentiments; for example, the

mother foresees that Henry will meet a girl at Schwaning's; Henry himself, just as he is on the verge of leaving his city, foresees the entire journey that awaits him; he feels "rapturous prophecies" (104) when he meets Mathilda. These presentiments are operative to such an extent that, whatever happens, the characters feel that they have already experienced it. In this world where temporal progression has no more relevance, there is no longer any such thing as original experience. Repetition is primary; the feeling of foreknowledge has been generalized. "When the old man had finished, it seemed to Henry that he had heard the song somewhere before" (75). The same feeling on Kling-sohr's part can be explained at least to some extent by Henry's familiarity with the hermit's book: the various forms of parallelism motivate each other interdependently.

4. *Allegorism*. The tendency toward allegory, that is, the constraints imposed upon readers that prevent us from settling for the first meaning of the words we read but that impel us rather to look for a second meaning, was a conscious one on Novalis's part, for in his drafts he spoke of an "allegorical territory" (*Schriften,* 339) and of "allegorical figures" (340). Tieck referred to "allegorical nature" (367) and concluded that "everything flows together in an allegory" (369). This was such a concern, in fact, that Novalis himself added the cautionary note: "But not too heavily allegorical" (342).

While it is implicit elsewhere, allegory imposes itself with special force in Klingsohr's tale, where it is marked in several ways. One obvious index is the choice of proper names: as in allegorical personifications, the characters are called Eros, the scribe, Fable, Dawn, Sun, Moon, Gold, Zinc, and so on. Another more diffuse index is the very difficulty we have understanding the tale's development if we limit ourselves to its literal meaning. The role of the supernatural (paradigmatic incoherence) and the bizarre nature of the story's transitions (syntagmatic incoherence) here play the role of allegorical indices, and oblige us to set out on an interpretive track that is independent of the principal semantic line.

At this point, it seems to me, we may take the convergence of the two oppositions – between genres and between men – for granted. We still need to ask whether the term *poetic* is fitting, or, from another viewpoint, we need to inquire into the textual reason for the inclusion of all these devices. We can say at the outset that no one of them is specifically poetic in itself, at least if we confine ourselves to their general description. The devices of embedding and parallelism in particular are readily found in the most novelistic (or narrative) of novels. Only the combined action of the four textual properties we have identified (among others) produces this impression. These properties are mutually determining. They invite interpretation of one sort rather than another; by virtue of their common presence, they point in a single direction. These devices are poetic, if at all, only through what unites them. We need to remember, too, that what I am analyzing here is my own intuition of the poetic, not Novalis's (though the two may well coincide).

I find not one but two common denominators, moreover, for the four properties. First, the reign of logico-temporal relations among phenomena has been abolished, replaced by an order of "correspondences." The governing principle in *Henry von Ofterdingen* is the opposite of the one Novalis called "wearisome and without visible goal . . . – the way of experience" (*Ofterdingen*, 29) or again "the unbroken chain of events" (93) that governs "hero" novels, narrative novels. Novalis achieves his effect in several ways: (a) through parallelisms (resemblance belongs to poets, difference to heroes); (b) through the way actions are linked; and (c) through the digressions introduced by embedding. Second, all representations tend to be undone. While a (static) description of the perceptible world would escape the thrust of the first series of devices, description and narration – and thus all fiction – become transparent, diluted. this effect is created principally by the general discussions in the text (assumed by the author or the characters), by the poems, and, in another way, by the tendency toward allegory. Here the difference is situated at the level of the reading contract that binds the reader to the text: a poetic reading entails its own rules, and, unlike the rules for fiction, these do not imply the construction of an imaginary universe.

Klingsohr declared that "poetry is the peculiar mode of activity of the human mind" (116), leaving no room for any other genre alongside poetry; but he also added that "a poet who should at the same time be a hero is an envoy from heaven" (114). Here is a way of rediscovering difference: the literary genres turn out to be the textual projection of the diversity of human attitudes to life.

6 Poetry without Verse

My title implies a question: What remains of poetry if verse is removed? It has been well understood since classical times that rhyme and meter alone do not add up to poetry: scientific treatises written in verse provide evidence. The question is not so simple, however, when we seek to formulate it in positive terms. If poetry is not verse, what is it? A corollary question arises from the difficulty we encounter in answering the first. Is there such a thing as transcultural and transhistoric "poeticity," or are there only localized solutions, circumscribed in time and space?

In discussing this problem, let us begin by considering the prose poem. Now the opposite of verse is prose; once we rule out verse, we may ask what the opposite of poetry is, and move on from there to a definition of the poetic. Here we have ideal experimental conditions, as it were, for our quest.

If the prose poem is the ideal place to seek an answer to questions about the nature of "verseless poetry," we would do well to begin by looking at previous work in this area, in particular Suzanne Bernard's impressive history and encyclopedia of the genre, *Le poème en prose de Baudelaire à nos jours*.[1] One chapter, "Esthetics of the Prose Poem," is entirely devoted to that question.

For Suzanne Bernard, the essence of the genre is perfectly represented in its oxymoronic label. "The entire complex set of laws that preside over the organization of this original genre are already potentially present in its very name: *prose poem*. . . . In fact, the prose poem, not only in its form but in its essence, is based on the union of opposites: prose and poetry, freedom and rigor, destructive anarchy and organizing art" (434). The author of a prose poem "aims at a static perfection, at a state of order and equilibrium – or else at an anarchic disorganization of the universe, at the heart of which he can bring forth another universe, recreate a world" (444).

What is in question here is still the prose poem, not verseless poetry. A cautionary remark is called for, however, for it concerns a characteristic feature of Bernard's discourse. It is one thing to assert that the prose poem is characterized by the encounter of opposites; it is something else again to say that

[1] Suzanne Bernard, *Le poème en prose de Baudelaire à nos jours* (Paris: Nizet, 1959).

a prose poem can be governed sometimes by one principle, sometimes by its opposite (for example, a tendency either to organization or to disorganization). The first assertion has a precise cognitive content and can be confirmed or disproved by the study of examples, as we shall see; the second has no precise content. A and $not\text{-}A$ divide up the universe exhaustively, so that to say of an object that it is characterized either by A or by $not\text{-}A$ is to say nothing at all. Now Bernard moves without transition from one assertion to another, as we noted in the passages quoted, which open and close the first part of her discussion.

But let us move on to the subject that interests us specifically, the definition of poetry. After explaining what prose consists of (realism, modernity, humor – we shall set aside these identifications as well), Bernard turns to the definition of a poem. Its first and principal feature is unity: we have a "definition of the poem as a *whole* whose essential features are unity and concentration" (439); "everything 'works' aesthetically, everything contributes to the overall impression, everything is indissolubly tied together in this poetic universe that is at once tightly unified and very complex"; we have "a set of relations, a highly organized universe" (441).

For the contemporary reader, these statements about unity, totality, and coherence are familiar; we are accustomed to seeing them attributed to structures in general, however, rather than being confined to poems. We might add that if not every structure is necessarily poetic, not every poem is necessarily structured, in this sense of the world. The ideal of organic unity is that of romanticism, but we may not be able to force every "poem" into it without doing violence either to the text or to the metatext, that is to critical vocabulary. I shall return to this point shortly.

Recognizing that the definition in terms of unity is a little too general (after all, is not the novel also "a highly organized universe"?), Bernard then invokes a second feature of the poem, an amplification of the first feature that allows us to distinguish poetry from other literary genres: this is a certain relation to time, or more precisely a way of escaping its hold. "The poem presents itself as a whole, an indivisible synthesis. . . . We are thus reaching a basic, essential requirement of the poem: it can only exist as a poem on condition that it restore the longest possible durations to the 'eternal present' of art, that it coagulate a moving process in atemporal forms – thereby converging with the requirements of musical form" (442).

If these statements are not perfectly transparent, if we should wish to know what linguistic realities are at issue, we find out that this particular atemporality is the common denominator of two series of devices. At the beginning of the first series, we find the principle that also underlies rhyme and rhythm (which are now absent), repetition, which imposes "a rhythmic structure on the *real time* of the work" (451). In the second set of devices, time is not suspended but abolished, either through the telescoping of different moments or by the destruction of logical categories (a distinction which is no sooner made than questioned, since Bernard adds, underlining the words, "which amounts to the same thing" [455]). This latter category (if it is a single category) is revealed in contexts where the poet "leaps brutally from one idea to another," "lacks transitions" (455), disperses "the connections, the linking of ideas, all consistency in description, all coherence in the narrative: modern poets, after Rimbaud, are installed in the discontinuous the better to deny the real universe" (456).

Let us overlook the fact that incoherence is presented here as a subdivision, a special feature of coherence itself, of unity or totality (through the intermediary of the "eternal present"). And let us postpone the empirical examination of these assertions. By limiting ourselves for the moment to the definition of poetry alone, we obtain its equivalence with timelessness. But the "devices" for producing this atemporal state – or rather, the processes that may have timelessness as their *consequence* (repetitions, incoherence) – can be reduced only quite hypothetically to this single common consequence! The deduction that makes it possible to subsume repetitions and incoherence under the notion of timelessness is as fragile as the syllogisms with which the "theater of the absurd" has familiarized us: men are mortal, mice are mortal, thus men are mice. It would be more prudent and more precise to leave aside the lofty principles of unity and timelessness, which teach us nothing, and reformulate Suzanne Bernard's thesis as follows: the poetic is sometimes conveyed by repetitions, and sometimes by verbal incoherence. This is perhaps accurate – it can be verified – but it does not give a single unified definition of poetry.

To examine the empirical validity of these hypotheses, let us now look at some actual prose poems, where the idea of poetry is at work. Two of the best known authors of prose poems can help us in this quest.

It is natural to begin with Baudelaire. He is not the inventor of the form; this is widely recognized today (assuming that the notion of *inventor* has a meaning), but it is he who assured its status, who introduced it onto the horizon of his contemporaries and his followers, who made it a model of writing: a genre, in the historical sense of the word. It is he too who popularized the very expression *poème en prose,* since he used it to designate the first published collections. The hope of finding an answer to our question grows stronger when we read, in the volume's dedication, that he dreamed of "the miracle of a poetic prose, musical without rhythm and without rhyme"[2]: this promised music of the signified is only a terminological variant of "poetry without verse."

Baudelaire puts the question well. However, the response given by the texts of the collection is somewhat disappointing, at least on first reading. For Baudelaire does not really write verseless poetry, does not simply seek the music of meaning. Instead, he writes poems-in-prose, that is, texts which, in their very essence, exploit the confrontation of opposites (and for this reason it may be argued that the collection, whose title was a subject of hesitation

[2] Charles Baudelaire, *Paris Spleen, 1869,* trans. Louise Varèse (New York: New Directions [James Laughlin], 1970) ix.

for Baudelaire, deserves rather to be called *Petits Poèmes en prose* rather than *Spleen de Paris,* even if the titles are somehow synonymous). It is as if Baudelaire had drawn the thematics and the structure of nine-tenths of these texts from the name of the genre, *poetic-prosaic,* or, shifting to a less nominalist version, as if he had only been attracted to the genre to the extent that it allowed him to find an adequate form (a "correspondence") for a thematics of duality, contrast, opposition; thus he offers a good illustration of Bernard's definition of the genre.

This assertion can be strengthened if we recall, first of all, the three different forms or figures the exploration of duality takes on. The first figure deserves the name of *implausibility* (Baudelaire himself spoke of "bizarreness"); a single phenomenon is described, but it is so out of tune with ordinary habits that we cannot keep from contrasting it with "normal" phenomena or events. Miss Bistoury is as strange a young woman as can be found, and the devil's generosity surpasses all expectations ("The Generous Gambler"). The superior gift is refused ("The Fairies' Gifts"), and a mistress's perfection leads to her murder ("Portraits Of Mistresses"). Sometimes this contrast makes it possible to oppose the subject of the enunciation to his contemporaries: the latter profess a naive humanism, the former believes that pain must be inflicted pain to awaken dignity ("Beat Up The Poor").

The second figure is *ambivalence.* Two opposing terms are both present here, but they characterize one and the same object. Sometimes, in a more or less rational way, ambivalence can be explained as the contrast between what things are and what they appear to be: a gesture that appeared to be noble is churlish ("Counterfeit," "The Rope"), a certain image of woman is the truth underlying a different image ("The Wild Woman And The Fashionable Coquette"). But most often the object itself has a dual aspect, in its appearance as in its essence: a woman is at once ugly and attractive ("A Thoroughbred"), ideal and hysterical ("Which Is The Real One?"), a man loves a woman and at the same time wants to kill her ("The Gallant Marksman"), or he incarnates cruelty and at the same time aspires to beauty ("The Bad Glazier"), a room is at once dream and reality ("The Double Room"). Certain places or moments take on value from the very fact that they can embody ambiguity: for instance, dusk, where day meets night ("Evening Twilight"), or a port, where action and contemplation merge ("Sea-Ports").

The third and last figure of duality, by far the most amply represented, is *antithesis,* the juxtaposition of two beings, phenomena, actions, or reactions that are endowed with contradictory qualities. Thus we have man and beast ("A Wag"), man and nature ("Cake"), rich men and poor ("Widows," "The Eyes Of The Poor"), joy and suffering ("The Old Clown"), crowds and isolation ("Crowds," "Solitude"), life and death ("The Shooting Gallery And The Cemetery"), time and eternity ("The Clock"), heaven and earth ("The Stranger"). Or else, as with the figures of implausibility, two contradictory reactions to the same phenomenon will be set side by side; often one is that of the crowd, while the other belongs to the poet: joy and disappointment

("Already!"), happiness and unhappiness ("The Desire To Paint"), love and hate ("The Eyes Of The Poor"), rejection and acceptance ("The Temptations"), admiration and fright ("Artist's Confiteor"), and so on.

This antithetical juxtaposition can in turn be experienced in a tragic or happy mode: even people who resemble each other reject each other ("The Old Woman's Despair"), even a second child "so exactly like the first one that I took them to be twins" engages with the other in a "war, literally fratricidal" (*Paris Spleen*, "Cake," 29). But from another point of view, the rich child and the poor one, although separated by "symbolic bars," turn out to be linked by their teeth, "of *identical* whiteness" ("The Poor Child's Toy," 36). In the aftermath of a brutal attack on an old beggar who gives him his own back, the "I" can declare: "Sir, *you are my equal!*" ("Beat Up The Poor," 102). And even though dreams may be the opposite of reality, they may become just as real ("Projects," "Windows").

This constant duality is not found in the work's general composition or its thematic structure alone. We have already observed how many titles are made up of juxtaposed opposites: "Venus And The Motley Fool," "The Dog And The Scent-Bottle," "The Wild Woman And The Fashionable Coquette," "The Soup And The Clouds," "The Shooting Gallery And The Cemetery." Others refer explicitly to duality (not to mention those that discover it in objects like the port, or dusk): for instance, "The Double Room," "Which Is The Real One?," "The Mirror." Whole sentences are often poised between two contrary terms: "delectable and execrable wife," "so many pleasures, so many pains" ("The Gallant Marksman," 90), "package of excrement" and "delicate perfumes" ("The Dog And The Scent-Bottle," 11). Or statements like these, one after another, in "The Old Clown": "Everywhere joy, money-making, debauchery; everywhere the assurance of tomorrow's daily-bread; everywhere frenetic outbursts of vitality. Here absolute misery, and a misery made all the more horrible by being tricked out in comic rags..." (26). Or these, in "Crowds": "Multitude, solitude: identical terms, and interchangeable by the active and fertile poet. The man who is unable to people his solitude is equally unable to be alone in a bustling crowd" (20). Entire texts are constructed around perfect symmetries: thus "The Double Room" consists of nineteen paragraphs, nine for the dream, nine for the reality, separated by a paragraph that begins "But...". Likewise in "Venus And The Motley Fool," we find three paragraphs devoted to joy, three to suffering, and a seventh in the middle that says: "Yet, in the midst of all this universal joy I caught sight of a grief-stricken soul" (10). Even the dedication of the collection illustrates – more than it theorizes – this constant encounter between contraries, as we slip, within a single paragraph, from poetic form to the theme of the big city, both viewed by Baudelaire as the constitutive feature of the prose poem.

The regularity of these contrasts is such that we end up forgetting that we are dealing with contrasts, with contradictions, with potentially tragic rips and tears. For Baudelaire, antithesis is enfolded in a system of correspondences, and not only because the oxymoronic prose poem corresponds perfectly to the contradictions it is to evoke. Whatever object or feeling is described, in the end it is integrated into a plurality of echoes, such as the woman, "allegorical dahlia," for whom, in "*L'Invitation au voyage*," the poet dreams of finding a frame-country that would resemble her: "Would you not there be framed within your own analogy, would you not see yourself reflected there in your own *correspondence,* as the mystics say?" (33). We may admire the multiplicity of resemblances: the four-term analogy (the woman is to the country what the portrait is to its frame) is reinforced by a similarity between contiguous objects: the frame must resemble the portrait, and the country must resemble the woman; and we must not forget that the portrait is indeed the portrait of the woman, that it is her faithful image (a direct resemblance between the frame of the painting and the country is all that is missing). Such a superlative "correspondence" is hardly exceptional in the poetic universe of Baudelaire, whether verse or prose, and it doubtless constitutes a good illustration of what Suzanne Bernard called "a set of relations, a highly organized universe." The fact remains nevertheless that the confrontation of contraries is precisely what unifies the Baudelairean collection.

The relationship between prose poem and thematic contrast is not confined to this structural resemblance alone. As we know, many of the poems take the poet's work as their object, thus adding the relation of participation to the relation of similarity: "Artist's Confiteor," "The Dog And The Scent-Bottle," "Crowds," "The Old Clown," "The Temptations," "The Desire To Paint," "Loss Of A Halo," and many others. Even more remarkably, the contrast evoked is made up precisely of the "prosaic" and the "poetic" – understood this time not as literary categories but as dimensions of life and the world. The man who dreams of clouds, while others seek to bring him down to earth, nearer to the prosaic soup – is he not a poet ("The Soup And The Clouds," "The Stranger")? Does not living as a poet mean living in illusion ("Although I may be a poet, I am not such a dupe as you would like to believe" ["The Wild Woman And The Fashionable Coquette," 19])? Living like those carefree wanderers, free from material attachments, who are admired by the young child whose spokesman – the poet – says: "For an instant I had the strange idea that I might, unknown to me, have a brother" ("Vocations," 71)? Is not the "horrible burden" of life precisely opposed to the intoxication of "wine, . . . poetry, or . . . virtue" ("Get Drunk," 74)? And is it not the prose of life to which one devotes all day, while hoping, in the middle of the night, to be able to balance it with a purely poetic activity: "You, dear God! grant me grace to produce a few beautiful verses to prove to myself that I am not the lowest of men" ("One O'Clock In The Morning," 14)?

One prose poem, "The Thyrsus," affirms this continuity between the thematic and formal levels with particular forcefulness. The thyrsus is an object, a stick, used in religious ceremonies. Its dual nature, though quite ordinary, is the starting point of the text, in which the thyrsus is first described "in its religious and poetic sense," then "physically" (72). The thyrsus is thus an ambivalent object, like the sea-port, like twilight, since it is poetic and spiritual on the one hand, prosaic and material on the other. Next a second antithesis is added, that of the straight line and the curve. Then, as if the relationship with poetry and art were not clear enough, as if the structural analogy did not suffice, there follows a direct equation: the thyrsus is the work of the artist himself. "The thyrsus is the image of your astonishing duality, great and venerated master" (the text is dedicated to Liszt). "Straight line and arabesque, intention and expression, inflexibility of the will, sinuosity of the word, unity of the goal, variety of the means, all-powerful and indivisible amalgam of genius, what analyst would have the detestable courage to divide and separate you!" (73). Material and spiritual, the thyrsus belongs first of all to prose and poetry; then, as a fusion of the straight line and the curve, it becomes the symbol of content and form in art – content and form in turn being ideally prolonged in the prosaic and the poetic. Can one conceive of a better symbol of the prose poem itself than the thyrsus?

Here lies the unity of Baudelaire's collection of prose poems, and of the notion of poetry these texts convey. This notion is by no means surprising: the poetic is envisaged here only in its contradictory union with prose, and it is nothing more than a synonym of the dream, the ideal, the spiritual – one is tempted to say, without any tautology, "of poetry." If we are to believe Baudelaire himself, then, the poetic is purely a thematic category to which is added the requirement of brevity. A text which may otherwise be narrative as well as descriptive, abstract or concrete, must, if it is to be poetic, remain brief; Baudelaire perceived this rule of Poe's as a constitutive feature of the genre ("we can cut wherever we please, I am dreaming, you your manuscript, the reader his reading; for I do not keep the reader's restive mind hanging in suspense on the thread of an interminable and superfluous plot," said the book's dedication [ix]). The poem is short; the poetic is ethereal; this would be all if we did not have to add the "work" of the correspondences we have already noted, a "work" which is as much involved in the *Petits poèmes en prose* as in *Les Fleurs du mal*. Through this last feature, we may see Baudelaire illustrating Bernard's first hypothesis, the one that identified the poetic with submission to the principle of resemblance.

But let us take a second example, historically and aesthetically close to Baudelaire: Rimbaud's *Illuminations*.[3] These are texts written in prose, yet their poetic character is unmistakable. Even if Rimbaud himself does not label them "poems in prose," his readers do, and that suffices to justify introducing them into our discussion.

Let us begin with a negative observation: Rimbaud's writing is not governed by the principle of resemblance that we have seen at work in Baudelaire. Metaphor, the master trope in Baudelaire's work, is virtually absent here. Similes, when they are present, bring to light no similarities: they are totally

---

[3] Arthur Rimbaud, *Illuminations and Other Prose Poems*, trans. Louise Varèse, rev. ed. (New York: New Directions [James Laughlin], 1957).

unmotivated comparisons. "The sea of the vigil, like Emily's breasts" ("Vigils," III, 77): but we know nothing whatsoever about Emily, so we shall never know what the sea of the vigil is like. "It is as simple as a musical phrase" ("War," 133): but the musical phrase is not, so far as we know, an embodiment of simplicity, and besides, the text that precedes this comparison and is supposedly illuminated by it is far from simple in its own right. "Wisdom . . . as scorned as chaos" ("Lives," I, 29): here are two opposites united by the scorn they evoke. "Pride more compassionate than the lost charities" ("Genie," 137): again two unknown entities brought together through the mediation of a third. Far from contributing to the establishment of a universe based on a universal analogy, these comparisons bring to light the incoherence of the world evoked.

The determined seeker of tropes in Rimbaud will find metonymies that do not create a world of correspondences. It is not even certain we are dealing with metonymies, for it might be argued that, just as the parts of the body or the properties of objects that one is at first tempted to interpret through synecdoche finally turn out to be literal parts and properties, referring to no totality, in the same way this dislocated and truncated world that Rimbaud's expressions evoke literally requires no ordering substitution. There is a great temptation, nonetheless, to sense an appeal to the metonymic imagination, even if the end point of the metonymy cannot always be confidently identified. When we read "our jargon muffles the drum" ("Democracy," 129), our linguistic habits lead us to transpose: language stands for speech, the instrument for the sound it makes; in a second phase, each of these actions evokes its agent. When we hear of "sands washed by the vinous sky" ("Metropolitan," 97) or "the mold of the ridge . . . trampled by all the homicides and all the battles" ("Mystic," 79), we have the impression once again that the use of metonymies involving an agent and an action or a place of action does have something to do with the obscurity of the passage.

One very well known stylistic characteristic of Rimbaud's text can also be related to its metonymic thrust: the poet describes optical illusions as if they were realities. An object near the top of a painting rises; if it is near the bottom, it falls. Yet do we not have metonymy in this passage from the image to the represented object, by way of contiguity and not resemblance? Thus, in the wood, "there is a cathedral that goes down and a lake that goes up" ("Childhood," III, 11); "above the level of the highest peaks, a sea, troubled . . ." appears ("Cities," 63); "they are playing cards at the bottom of the pond" ("Historic Evening," 113); the metamorphosis is motivated in "After The Deluge": "the sea, high tiered as in old prints" (3). I take metonymy again to be responsible for expressions such as "steel" pastures ("Mystic," 79), "tricolored" eyes ("Parade," 21), "spicy plains" ("Lives," I, 29), "bleak land" (*campagne aigre*) and "beggar childhood" ("Lives," II, 31), the "eyes full of pilgrimages" ("Childhood," I, 9). Or these strange statements: "Rolands trumpet their valor" ("Cities," 61), "operatic scenes . . . look down" ("Scenes,"

109–111), "the lamps and the rugs of the vigil make the noise of waves" ("Vigils," III, 77), "I note the story of the treasures you discovered" ("Lives," I, 29).

Rimbaud's *Illuminations* are poetic, then, not because they are "highly organized," in the sense that this expression could have in the Baudelairean context, or because of their metaphoric character (metonymy is reputed to be prosaic). Moreover, this is not what is usually attributed to them. As we have seen, Bernard articulated the second fundamental tendency of Rimbaud's prose poem: incoherence, discontinuity, the negation of the real universe. In a word, we may say that Rimbaud's text rejects representation; and this is how it is poetic. But such an assertion requires some explanation, in particular concerning the representative character of literary texts.

In his *Correspondance des arts,* Etienne Souriau posed the problem of representation in art quite explicitly, by making it a distinctive typological feature.[4] For in fact, alongside the representative arts, there are others which are not representative, and which Souriau calls "presentative." "To the sonata-being or the cathedral-being are inherent, as to their subject, all the attributes, morphological and other, that contribute to their structure. Whereas in the representative arts, there is a sort of ontological doubling – a plurality of these subjects of inherence. . . . It is this duality of the ontological subjects of inherence – on the one hand the work, on the other the objects represented – which characterizes the representative arts. In the representative arts, work and object converge. The representative work gives rise, so to speak, alongside itself and outside itself (at least outside its body and beyond its phenomena, although still emanating from itself and supported by itself), to a world of beings and things that cannot be confused with it" (89). The result is a major division of the arts into "two distinct groups," "the group of arts in which the universe of the work posits beings ontologically distinct from the work itself; and that of the arts in which the object-oriented interpretation of the data interprets the work without supposing in it anything other than itself" (90).

When Souriau turns toward the literary realm, however, he is obliged to note an assymetry in his tableau of "artistic correspondence": no "presentative" or first-degree literature really exists. The primary form of literature would be "the arabesque of the consonants and vowels, their 'melody,' . . . their rhythm and, more broadly, the general gesture of the sentence, of the period, the succession of periods, and so on" (154). This "primary slot (which would theoretically include an art of the more or less musical assemblage of syllables without any signifying intention, thus without any representative evocation) is virtually vacant – except for a 'pure prosody' which does not exist as an autonomous art: it is only implied in poetry, as a primary form of an art that is actually of the second degree" (132). Such a pertinence of the signifier indeed makes it possible to oppose poetry to prose (this is how Souriau answers the

[4] Étienne Souriau, *Correspondance des arts: éléments d'esthétique comparée,* 2nd ed. (Paris: Flammarion, 1969).

question I am asking in these pages [158]), but to all appearances it plays only a rather marginal role in relation to literature as a whole: the dadaists' *Laut-dichtung,* the futurists' neologisms, lettrist or concrete poetry. The reason for this, according to Souriau, is the musical poverty of the sounds of language, compared to music as such; and one might add, the visual poverty of letters, compared to the set of means available to painting.

All this seems quite accurate, and yet one begins to regret that the presen-tation/representation dichotomy, applied to the literary realm, produces such limited results. So much so that one may wonder whether the interpretation of this dichotomy is indeed the one that is appropriate to the field of literature, and whether it does not square better with what is only raw material for literature, namely, language. Souriau himself writes: "Literature . . . borrows its entire set of signs from a system that has already been fully constituted apart from itself: language" (154). The "primary form" of literature is not sounds, but words and phrases, and these already have signifiers *and* signifieds. "Presentative" literature would be not only that in which the signifier ceases to be transparent and transitive, but that literature, much more important quantitatively and qualitatively, in which the signified also ceases to be trans-parent and transitive. It would thus be a matter of calling into question the automatic linking that I referred to above ("without any signifying intent, *thus* without any intent of representative evocation"), in order to find out whether there may not exist a form of writing that includes signification but not rep-resentation. This literature of presentation is illustrated by Rimbaud's *Illu-minations,* whose poetry resides in their presentative character.

The means Rimbaud uses to destroy the representative illusion are quite numerous. They extend from explicit metalinguistic commentary, as in the famous sentence from "Barbarian": "The banner of raw meat against the silk of seas and arctic flowers (they do not exist)" (*Illuminations,* 101), to frankly agrammatical sentences, whose meaning will never be known, like the one with which "Metropolitan" concludes: "The morning when with Her you struggled among the glitterings of snow, those green lips, those glaciers, black banners and blue beams, and the purple perfumes of the polar sun. – Your strength" (99). Between these two extremes, a series of devices makes rep-resentation uncertain and eventually impossible.

Thus the indeterminate sentences that fill most of the *Illuminations* do not preclude all representation, but they make it extremely imprecise. When, at the end of "After The Deluge," Rimbaud says that "the Queen, the Witch who lights her fire in the earthen pot, will never tell us what she knows, and what we do not know" (5), we see a physical gesture carried out by a female character, but we know nothing whatever about this character or her rela-tionship with what precedes (the floods), and of course we do not know "what we do not know." In the same way we shall never know anything about the "two faithful children" of the "musical house," or the "single old man, hand-some and calm" mentioned in "Phrases" (45), or the other characters in *Il-luminations.* These beings come forth and disappear like celestial bodies in the middle of the dark night, in the flash of an illumination. Discontinuity has a similar effect: each word may evoke a representation, but taken together they do not make a whole, and we are thus led to settle for the words. "For Helen's childhood, furs and shadows trembled, and the breast of the poor and the legends of heaven" ("Fairy," 131): the very plurality of subjects poses a problem, for each one helps make its predecessor unreal. The same can be said of all the circumstantial complements in the sentence quoted from "Metropolitan," or of another sentence from the same text, in which there are "roads bordered by walls and iron fences," "dreadful flowers," "inns that now never open any more, – there are princesses, and if you are not too overwhelmed, the study of the stars – the sky" (99). This is perhaps why one is always tempted to permute words, in Rimbaud's texts, in an effort to find some coherence in them.

Other devices render representation not only uncertain but truly impossible. This is the case for oxymorons and contradictory sentences; also for the changing framework of enunciation, in which "I" and "you" (singular, familiar), "we" and "you" (plural, formal) are rarely maintained from one end of a text to the other (for example, in "After The Deluge," "Side Show," "Lives," "Morning of Drunkenness," "Metropolitan," "Dawn"). Is the "Being of Beauty" external or internal to the subject, the one that says at the end: "*our* bones are clothed with an amorous new body" ("Being Beauteous," 27; emphasis added)? The same is true of Rimbaud's already-mentioned tendency to describe properties or parts of objects without ever naming the objects themselves, to such an extent that one really cannot tell what is in question. This holds good not only for texts like *"H,"* which is presented like a real riddle, but also for countless others, as the critics' hesitations often attest. It is this attention to properties, at the expense of the objects they characterize, that gives us the impression that Rimbaud always prefers the generic term to the proper word, and imparts a strong tinge of abstraction to his text. What exactly is the "nocturnal extravagance" of "Vagabonds" (65), or the "incredible luxury" of "Phrases" (45)? The "ordinary generosities" or "revolutions of love" of "Tale" (17)? The "summer grass" and "serious vice" of "Devotions" (125)? "My discomfiture" and "this vile despair" of "Phrases" (47)? The "precious blazes" and the "cold influence" of "Fairy"? The "economic horrors" and "bourgeois magic" of "Historic Evening" (113, 115)? Rimbaud also has a penchant for universal quantifiers, as if he were a legislator: "people of all possible characters amidst all possible appearances" ("Vigils," II, 77), "all their characters were reflected in my face" ("War," 133), and so on.

Two arguments might be brought against this analysis of the failure of representation in *Illuminations*. First, it is not true that all the texts of *Illuminations,* and all the sentences in each text, share in this tendency: if representation often fails, it also often succeeds. Furthermore, the same verbal characteristics that contribute to this failure can be found outside of literature, and especially outside of poetry, in abstract and general texts in particular.

The response to these two objections is, fortunately, the same. The opposition between presentation and representation through language is not situated between two classes of utterances but between two categories. Language may be transparent or opaque, transitive or intransitive; but these are only two extreme poles, and concrete utterances are always located, as it were, somewhere between the two: they are only closer to, or farther from, one of the extremes. At the same time it is never an isolated category, and its combination with others is what makes the refusal of representation a source of poetry in *Illuminations*: the philosophical text, for example, that does not represent, maintains coherence at the level of its very meaning. It is indeed their "presentative" character that makes these texts poetic, and one might represent the typological system internalized by Rimbaud's readers – however unwittingly – as follows:

	Verse	Prose
presentation	poetry	prose poem
representation	epic, narration, and versified description	fiction (novel, tale)

Which brings us back to our starting point. Atemporality, which for Bernard constituted the essence of poeticity, is only a secondary consequence of the rejection of representation in Rimbaud, of the order of correspondences in Baudelaire; it would thus be a violent distortion of the facts to try to equate the one with the other. But even if the texts of two poets separated by a scant dozen years, writing in the same language and in the same intellectual climate of presymbolism, are qualified (by themselves or by their contemporaries) as "poetic" for such different, independent reasons, must we not bow to the evidence? Poetry in general does not exist, but variable conceptions of poetry exist and will continue to exist, not only from one period or country to another but also from one text to another. The presentation/representation opposition is universal and "natural" (it is inscribed in language); but the identification of poetry with the "presentative" use of language is a historically circumscribed and culturally determined fact: it leaves Baudelaire outside "poetry." What remains is to wonder – but we can see what preliminary work the response would imply – whether there may nonetheless be some affinity among all the different reasons for which, in the past, a text has been labeled poetic. Our limited objective in these pages has been to show that this affinity does not lie where it has been assumed to lie, and to offer a more precise formulation of some of the reasons for this.

PART THREE

7 *Notes from the Underground*

In a bookshop my hand just happened to come to rest on *L'Esprit souterrain,* [*Notes from the Underground*] a recent French translation. . . . The instinct of affinity (or what shall I call it?) spoke to me instantaneously – my joy was beyond bounds.
Friedrich Nietzsche[1]

I believe that with *Notes from the Underground* we reach the peak of Dostoevsky's career. I consider this book (and I am not alone) the capstone of his entire work.
André Gide[2]

Notes from the Underground . . . : no other text by Dostoevsky has exerted more influence on twentieth-century thought or technique. George Steiner[3]

Many more such testimonies could be cited, but there is hardly any need. The centrality of this text for Dostoevsky's work is a common-place today, paralleling its centrality in the Dostoevsky myth that characterizes our era.

Dostoevsky's reputation may be assured, but the same cannot be said for the exegesis of his work. Countless critical texts have been devoted to him, as one might expect; the problem is that they deal only rarely with Dostoevsky's texts. The man had the misfortune of living an eventful life. What erudite biographer could resist the attraction of the prison years, the passion for gambling, the epilepsy, the tumultuous love affairs? Biographers who get beyond this level face a second obstacle. Dostoevsky was passionately interested in the philosophical and religious problems of his time; he transmitted his passion to his characters so that his books are infused with it. Thus his critics rarely speak of "Dostoevsky-the-writer," as people used to say. They all focus enthusiastically on his "ideas," forgetting that these ideas come embedded in

---

[1] *Selected Letters of Friedrich Nietzsche,* ed. and trans. Christopher Middleton (Chicago and London: The University of Chicago Press, 1969) letter 149, to Franz Overbeck, February 23, 1887.
[2] *Dostoïevski: Articles et causeries* (Paris: Gallimard, 1923) 164–5.
[3] *Tolstoy or Dostoevsky: An Essay in the Old Criticism* (New York: Knopf, 1971).

novels. Furthermore, even if the biographers had adopted a different perspective, they could not have avoided the danger in its inverse form: one can hardly study Dostoevsky's "technique" without regard to the great ideological debates that animate his novels (Shklovksy claimed that *Crime and Punishment* was simply a detective novel with just one odd feature, namely that its suspense was induced by its interminable philosophical debates). To propose a reading of Dostoevsky today is in a sense to take up a challenge: one must manage to see Dostoevsky's "ideas" and his "technique" simultaneously, without unduly privileging one or the other.

Interpretive criticism (as distinguished from erudite criticism) habitually makes the mistake of declaring (1) that Dostoevsky is a *philosopher*, "literary form" notwithstanding, and (2) that Dostoevsky is *a* philosopher, whereas even the observer with the fewest possible preconceptions is struck at once by the diversity of the philosophical, moral, and psychological concepts that are juxtaposed in his work. As Bakhtin writes, at the beginning of a study to which we shall have occasion to return: "Any acquaintance with the voluminous literature on Dostoevsky leaves the impression that one is dealing not with a *single* author-artist who wrote novels and stories but with a number of philosophical statements by *several* author-thinkers. Raskolnikov, Myshkin, Stavrogin, Ivan Karamazov, the Grand Inquisitor, and others."[4]

More than any other of Dostoevsky's works except perhaps the "Legend of the Grand Inquisitor," *Notes from the Underground* is the text most responsible for the situation I have just described. This text has tended to give readers the impression of possessing direct testimony by Dostoevsky-the-ideologue. Thus we shall have to begin with this text if we wish to read Dostoevsky today, or, more generally, if we wish to understand his role in that endlessly changing whole we call *literature*.

Notes from the Underground is divided into two parts, called "Underground" and "A Propos of the Wet Snow."[5] Dostoevsky himself describes them as follows: "In this extract, entitled 'Underground,' the person introduces himself and his views and, as it were, tries to explain those causes which have not only led, but also were bound to lead, to his appearance in our midst. In the subsequent extract 'A Propos of the Wet Snow' we shall reproduce this person's *Notes* proper, dealing with certain events of his life" (107, note). It is in Part One, the narrator's plea for the defense, that readers have always found Dostoevsky's most "remarkable" ideas exposed. We too shall enter into the labyrinth of this text through Part One – without yet knowing where or how we shall be able to get out.

[4] Mikhaïl Bakhtin, *Problems of Dostoevsky's Poetics,* trans. Caryl Emerson (Minneapolis: University of Minnesota Press, 1984) 5.
[5] Cited from *The Best Short Stories of Dostoevsky,* trans. David Magarshack (New York: Random House, 1964).

The Narrator's Ideology

The first theme taken up by the narrator is consciousness (*soznanie*). In this context, the term is opposed not to the unconscious but to lack of self-consciousness. The narrator depicts two types of men: one is simple and direct (*neposredstvennyu*), *"l'homme de la nature et de la vérité"* ["the man of nature and truth"] in French in the text who, when he acts, possesses no image of his own action; the other is conscious man. For the latter, every action is accompanied by its image, arising in his consciousness. What is worse, the image appears before the action has taken place and thereby renders the action impossible. The man of consciousness cannot be the man of action. "For the direct, the inevitable, and the legitimate result of consciousness is to make all action impossible, or – to put it differently – consciousness leads to thumb-twiddling. . . . Let me repeat, and repeat most earnestly: all plain men and men of action are active only because they are dull-witted and mentally underdeveloped" (122).

As an example let us take the case of an insult that would "normally" lead to revenge. This is indeed how men of action behave. "They are, let us assume, so seized by the feeling of revenge that while that feeling lasts there is nothing but that feeling left in them. Such a man goes straight to his goal, like a mad bull, with lowered horns, and only a stone wall perhaps will stop him" (115). The same cannot be said of the man of consciousness. "I argued that a man revenges himself because he finds justice in it. This of course means that he has found a primary cause, a basis, namely, justice. . . . But I can't for the life of me see any justice here, and therefore if I should start revenging myself, it would merely be out of spite. Now spite, of course, could get the better of anything, of all my doubts, and so could very well take the place of any primary cause just because it is not a cause. But what can I do if I have not even spite . . . Besides, my feeling of bitterness, too, is subject to the process of disintegration as a result of those damned laws of consciousness. One look and the object disappears into thin air, your reasons evaporate, there is no guilty man, the injury is no longer an injury but just fate, something in the nature of toothache for which no one can be blamed, and consequently there is only one solution left, namely, knocking your head against the wall as hard as you can" (123).

The narrator begins by deploring this excess of consciousness ("I assure you, gentlemen, that to be too acutely conscious is a disease, a real, honest-to-goodness disease. It would have been quite sufficient for the business of everyday life to possess the ordinary human consciousness, that is to say, half or even a quarter of the share which falls to the lot of an intelligent man of our unhappy nineteenth century" [111]); but at the end of his argument he observes that excessive consciousness is nevertheless the lesser of evils: "And though at the beginning I did argue that consciousness was the greatest misfortune to man, yet I know that man loves it and will not exchange it for any satisfaction" (140). "And, finally, gentlemen, it is much better to do nothing at all! Better passive awareness!" (142).

The corollary to this assertion is the solidarity between consciousness and suffering. Consciousness provokes suffering, condemning man to inaction, but at the same time it results from suffering. "Suffering! Why, it's the sole cause of consciousness!" (140). Here a third term, *pleasure,* intervenes and we find ourselves confronting a very "Dostoevskyan" statement; for the time being, I shall simply present it without attempting an explanation. On several occasions, the narrator declares that at the heart of the greatest suffering, provided he becomes fully conscious of it, he will find a source of enjoyment, "pleasure that sometimes reaches the highest degree of voluptuousness" (120). Here is an example: "It got so far that I felt a sort of secret, abnormal, contemptible delight when, on coming home on one of the foulest nights in Petersburg, I used to realise intensely that again I had been guilty of some particularly dastardly action that day, and that once more it was no earthly use crying over spilt milk; and inwardly, secretly, I used to go on nagging myself, worrying myself, accusing myself, till at last the bitterness I felt turned into a sort of shameful, damnable sweetness, and finally, into real, positive delight! Yes, into delight! . . . Let me explain it to you. The feeling of delight was there just because I was so intensely aware of my own degradation; because I felt myself that I had come up against a blank wall; that no doubt, it was bad, but that it couldn't be helped . . . " (112–13). And in another passage: "And it is just in that cold and loathsome half-despair and half-belief – in that conscious burying oneself alive for grief for forty years – in that intensely perceived, but to some extent uncertain, helplessness of one's position – in all that poison of unsatisfied desires that have turned inwards – in that fever of hesitations, firmly taken decisions, and regrets that follow almost instantaneously upon them – that the essence of that delight I have spoken of lies" (116–17).

This suffering that conscious reckoning transforms into delight may also be purely physical, as for example with toothache. Here is the description of an "educated man" on the third day of his suffering: "His groans become nasty and offensively ill-tempered groans, and go on for days and nights. And yet he knows perfectly well that he is doing no good with his groaning; he knows better than anyone that he is merely irritating and worrying himself and others for nothing; he knows that the audience before whom he is performing with such zeal and all his family are listening to him with disgust, that they don't believe him in the least, and that in their hearts they know that, if he wished, he could have groaned differently and more naturally, without such trills and flourishes, and that he is only amusing himself out of spite and malice. Well, all those apprehensions and infamies are merely the expression of sensual pleasure" (120). This is what is called the *masochism* of the underground man.

Apparently without transition, the narrator moves on to his second major theme, reason, its role in man, and the value of behavior that attempts to conform exclusively to reason. The argument goes roughly as follows. (1) Reason can never know anything but the "reasonable," that is, only a "twentieth part" of the human being. (2) The essential part of the human being is constituted by desire, by the will, which is not reasonable. "What does reason know? Reason only knows what it has succeeded in getting to know (certain things, I suppose, it will never know; this may be poor comfort, but why not admit it frankly?), whereas human nature acts as a whole, with everything that is in it, consciously, and unconsciously, and though it may commit all sorts of absurdities, it persists" (133). "Reason is an excellent thing. There is no doubt about it. But reason is only reason, and it can only satisfy the reasoning ability of man, whereas volition is a manifestation of the whole of life, I mean, of the whole of human life, including reason with all its concomitant head-scratchings" (ibid.). (3) It is thus absurd to seek to establish a way of life – and impose it on others – on the basis of reason alone. "For instance, you want to cure man of his old habits and reform his will in accordance with the demands of science and common sense. But how do you know that man not only could but *should* be remade like that? And what leads you to conclude that human desires must *necessarily* be reformed? In short, how do you know that such a reformation will be a gain to man?" (140). Dostoevsky thus denounces the totalitarian determinism that underlies attempts to explain all human actions by referring to the laws of reason.

His own reasoning is based on arguments, and entails in turn certain conclusions. The arguments are of two sorts. Some are drawn from collective experience, from the history of humanity: the evolution of civilization has not brought about the reign of reason, there is as much absurdity in the modern world as in ancient society. "Well, just take a good look round you: rivers of blood are being spilt, and in the jolliest imaginable way, like champagne" (128). The other arguments derive from the narrator's personal experience: not all desires can be explained by reason; if they could be, man would have acted differently – deliberately, in defiance of reason; the theory of absolute determinism is therefore false; against that theory the narrator defends the right to act on impulse (this is what Gide takes from Dostoevsky). Moreover, the love of suffering is contrary to reason, yet it exists (as we saw earlier and as the narrator reminds us here: "And man does love suffering very much sometimes. He loves it passionately. That is an undeniable fact" [139–40]). There is finally one other argument, intended to ward off a potential objection. Is it not the case that the majority of human actions are directed, at all events, toward reasonable goals? Here the answer is yes, but only superficially. In fact, even in carrying out an apparently reasonable action, man obeys a different principle: he accomplishes the action for its own sake, and not to achieve a result. "The important point is not where [the path] leads but that it should lead somewhere" (138). "But man is a frivolous and unaccountable creature, and perhaps, like a chess-player, he is only fond of the *process* of achieving his aim, but not of the aim itself. And who knows (it is impossible to be absolutely sure about it), perhaps the whole aim mankind is striving to achieve on earth merely lies in this incessant process of achievement, or (to put it differently) in life itself, and not really in the attainment of any goal" (138–9).

The conclusions drawn from this assertion apply to all social reformers (including revolutionaries), for such people imagine that they know man inside out, and from what is in fact partial knowledge they have derived the image of an ideal society, a "crystal palace." Since their knowledge of man is inadequate, their conclusions are mistaken; consequently, what they offer him is not a palace but a tenement, even a hencoop, or an anthill. "You see, if it were not a palace but a hencoop, and if it should rain, I might crawl into it to avoid getting wet, but I would never pretend that the hencoop was a palace out of gratitude to it for sheltering me from the rain. You laugh and you tell me that in such circumstances even a hencoop is as good as a palace. Yes, I reply, it certainly is if the only purpose in life is not to get wet. . . . For the time being, however, I refuse to accept a hencoop for a palace" (141). Totalitarian determinism is not only erroneous, it is dangerous: by dint of viewing men as cogs in the machinery, or as "domestic animals," one risks leading them into such a condition. This is what is called Dostoevsky's *antisocialism* (his conservatism).

The Drama of Speech

If *Notes from the Underground* were limited to Part One, and if this part were limited to the ideas we have just been discussing, the book's reputation would be hard to account for. Not that the narrator's assertions are inconsistent; nor should they be viewed from the distorted perspective of today and denied any originality. More than one hundred years have gone by since the publication of the *Notes* (1864), and we have become too accustomed since then, perhaps, to think in terms approaching Dostoevsky's. Even so, the philosophical, ideological, and scientific value of the author's declarations alone certainly does not suffice to distinguish this book from countless others.

But authorial pronouncements are not what we read, when we open *Notes from the Underground*. What we encounter is not a collection of thoughts but a narrative, a work of fiction. Dostoevsky's first real innovation consists in the miracle of this metamorphosis. The issue here is not a simple opposition of form to content. The notion of overcoming the incompatibility between fiction and nonfiction, between the "mimetic" and the "discursive," is also an "idea," and one to be reckoned with. We have to resist the temptation to reduce the work to isolated statements taken out of context and attributed directly to Dostoevsky the thinker. Now that we are familiar with the substance of the arguments that are to be presented, we need to see how these arguments are conveyed. For instead of observing the straightforward presentation of an idea, we are going to witness its *enactment*. And as befits a dramatic situation, several *roles* will be available to us.

A first role is attributed to the texts invoked or cited. From the time of its first publication onward, *Notes from the Underground* has been perceived by the public as a polemical text. In the 1920s, V. Komarovich explicated most of the references he found dispersed or dissimulated in the work. The text refers to a set of ideological propositions that dominated Russian radical and liberal thinking between 1840 and 1870. The expression "the sublime and beautiful," always put in quotes, refers to Kant, Schiller, and German idealism; *l'homme de la nature et l'homme de la vérité* refers to Rousseau (whose role is somewhat more complex, as we shall see); the positivist historian Buckle is cited by name. But the most direct adversary is a Russian contemporary: Nikolaï Chernyshevsky, guru of the radical youth of the 1860s, author of a utopian and didactic novel entitled *What Is To Be Done?* as well as several theoretical articles, one of which is called "On the Anthropological Principle in Philosophy." It is Chernyshevsky who defends totalitarian determinism, in the article cited as well as through the intermediary of the characters in his novel (Lopoukhov in particular). It is he, too, who sets another character (Vera Pavlovna) to dreaming in the crystal palace, in a scene that refers indirectly to Fourier's phalanstery and to the writings of Fourier's Russian followers. At no point, then, is the text of *Notes from the Underground* simply the impartial exposition of an idea; we are given a polemical dialogue in which the other interlocutor was quite present in the minds of contemporary readers.

Alongside this first role, which we might call "they" (referring to earlier discourses by others), there appears a second, that of "you," or the represented interlocutor. This "you" appears in the very first sentence, more precisely in the suspension points that separate "I am a sick man" from "I am a spiteful man" (107): the tone changes between the first clause and the second because the narrator hears or anticipates a pitying reaction to his first statement and goes on to reject it in the second. Shortly afterward, "you" appears in the text: "I don't suppose you will understand that" (108). "But doesn't it seem to you, gentlemen, that I might possibly be apologising to you for something? Asking you to forgive me for something? Yes, I'm sure it does . . . " (109). "If, irritated with all this idle talk (and I feel that you are irritated), you were to ask me . . . " (110), and so forth.

This direct address to the imaginary listener and the formulation of his presumed responses is pursued throughout the book. However, the image of "you" does not remain stable. In the first six chapters of Part One, "you" simply denotes an average reaction, that of Everyman, who is listening to this fevered confession, is suspicious, irritated, and so forth. In the seventh chapter, however, and through chapter ten, the role is modified: "you" is no longer satisfied with a passive reaction, he takes a position and his interventions become as lengthy as the narrator's. We are familiar with this position: it belongs to "they" (let us say, to simplify things, that it is Chernyshevsky's). It is to "they" that the narrator now speaks when he declares: "You gentlemen have, so far as I know, drawn up your entire list of positive human values by taking the averages of statistical figures and relying on scientific and economic formulae" (126). It is to this second "you-they" that the narrator says: "You believe in the Crystal Palace, forever indestructible . . . " (140). Finally, in the last (eleventh) chapter, we return to the initial "you," and this "you" becomes at the same time thematized in the narrator's discourse: "Now, of course, I've made up all this speech of yours myself. It, too, comes from the dark cellar.

I've been listening to your words for forty years through a crack in the ceiling. I have invented them myself. It is the only thing I did invent" (144).

Finally, the last role in this drama belongs to "I," to an "I" that is of course doubled, for as we know, every appearance of "I," every naming of a speaker, posits a new enunciatory context in which it is another "I," not yet named, that is speaking. Here is at once the most powerful and the most original feature of this discourse: its aptitude to mix the linguistic freely with the metalinguistic, to contradict the one with the other, to pursue an infinite regression in the metalinguistic domain. Indeed, the explicit representation of the speaker allows for a series of figures. Here is the contradiction: "I was a spiteful civil servant" (108). On the next page: "Incidentally, I was rather exaggerating just now when I said that I was a spiteful civil servant" (109). The metalinguistic commentary: "I was rude and took pleasure in being rude. Mind you, I never accepted any bribes, so that I had at least to find something to compensate myself for that. (A silly joke, but I shan't cross it out. I wrote it thinking it would sound very witty, but now that I have seen myself that I merely wanted to indulge in a bit of contemptible bragging, I shall let it stand on purpose!)" (108). Or in another passage: "Let me continue calmly about the people with strong nerves . . . " (117). Self-refutation: "I assure you most solemnly, gentlemen, that there is not a word I've just written I believe in!" (143). Infinite regression (an example from Part Two): "Of course, on the other hand, you are quite right. As a matter of fact, it is mean and contemptible. And what is even meaner is that now I should be trying to justify myself to you. Enough of this, though, or I should never finish: things are quite sure to get meaner and meaner anyway" (164). And the entire eleventh chapter of Part One is devoted to the problem of writing: Why write? For whom? The explanation the narrator proposes (he writes for himself, to get rid of his painful memories) is in fact only one among several that are suggested at other levels of rereading.

The drama that Dostoevsky staged in *Notes* is the drama of speech, with its perennial protagonists: the present discourse, "this"; the absent discourses of others, "they"; the "you" of the addressee, always ready to turn itself into a speaker; and finally the "I" of the subject of the enunciation – which appears only when an enunciation enunciates it. The utterance, caught up in this play, loses all stability, all objectivity, all impersonality. Absolute ideas, the intangible crystallizations of a forever-forgotten process, have ceased to exist; ideas have become as fragile as the world around them.

The new status of ideas is one of the very points clarified in Bakhtin's study of Dostoevsky's poetics (a study that picks up on remarks by several earlier Russian critics: Ivanov, Grossman, Askoldov, Engelgardt). In the non-Dostoevskyan novelistic world, which Bakhtin calls monologic, ideas can have two functions. They may express the opinion of the author (and be attributed to a character only for convenience); or, if they are ideas to which the author no longer adheres, they may serve as psychic or social characteristics of a character (by metonymy). But as soon as an idea is taken seriously, it no longer belongs to anyone. "Everything [in a plurality of consciousnesses] that is essential and true is incorporated into the unique context of 'consciousness in general' and deprived of its individuality. That which is individual, that which distinguishes one consciousness from another and from others, is cognitively not essential and belongs to the realm of an individual human being's psychical organization and limitation. From the point of view of truth, there are no individual consciousnesses. Idealism recognizes only one principle of cognitive individualization: *error*. True judgments are not attached to a personality, but correspond to some unified, systematically monologic context. Only error individualizes."[6]

According to Bakhtin, Dostoevsky's "Copernican revolution" consists precisely in his annihilation of the impersonality and solidity of ideas. Here ideas are always "interindividual and intersubjective." "His form-shaping world-view does not know an *impersonal truth* and in his works there are no detached, impersonal verities" (96). In other words, ideas lose their singular, privileged status; they cease to be immutable essences and instead are integrated in a broader circuit of signification, in an immense symbolic game. For earlier literature (obviously such a generalization is unfair), ideas are pure signifieds; they *are signified* (by words or acts) but do not *signify* themselves (except as psychological characteristics). For Dostoevsky and to varying degrees some of his contemporaries (like the Nerval of *Aurélia*), ideas are not the *result* of a process of symbolic representation, they are an integral *part* of it. Dostoevsky removes the discursive/mimetic opposition by giving ideas the role not only of *symbolized* but also of *symbolizer*; he transforms the idea of representation not by rejecting or limiting it but, quite to the contrary (although the results may look the same), by extending it into areas that had previously been foreign to it. In Pascal's *Pensées,* as in *Notes from the Underground,* one can find observations about a heart that reason does not know; but one cannot imagine the *Pensées* transformed into an "internal dialogue" in which the voice that is making pronouncements at the same time denounces itself, contradicts itself, accuses itself of lying, judges itself ironically, makes fun of itself – and of us.

When Nietzsche says of Dostoevsky that "I prize his work ... as the most valuable psychological material known to me,"[7] he is taking part in a secular tradition that reads the psychological, the philosophical, and the social in the literary realm – but not literature itself, or discourse; a tradition that fails to see that Dostoevsky's innovation is far greater on the symbolic than on the psychological level, which here is only one element among others. Dostoevsky alters our ideas of ideas and our representation of representation.

But is there a relation between this theme *of* dialogue and the themes evoked *in* the dialogue? ... Perhaps the labyrinth has not yet disclosed all its secrets. Let us try another path, by plunging into a still unexplored zone: the second

[6] Bakhtin, *Problems of Dostoevsky's Poetics,* 81.
[7] *Selected Letters,* letter 187, to Georg Brandes, November 20, 1888.

part of the book. Who knows, perhaps the indirect path will turn out to be the faster.

Part Two is more traditionally narrative; still, it does not exclude the elements of the drama of speech that we have observed in Part One. "I" and "you" behave as before, but "they" changes and takes on greater importance. Rather than entering into a dialogue or polemic – thus into a syntagmatic relation – like the earlier texts, the narrative takes the form of *parody* (a paradigmatic relation), by imitating and overturning the situations of earlier narratives. In a sense, *Notes from the Underground* has the same goal as *Don Quixote*: to make fun of a certain contemporary literature, attacking it as much through parody as through open polemics. The role played by chivalry novels in Cervantes's text is played in Dostoevsky's by Russian and Western Romantic literature in two different ways. On the one hand, the hero participates in situations that parody the peripeties of Chernyshevsky's *What Is To Be Done,* for example, in the meetings with the officer or with Lisa. Lopoukhov, in Chernyshevsky's novel has the habit of never giving way in the street except to women and old men; when on one occasion a rude character fails to stand aside, Lopoukhov, a man of great physical strength, simply shoves him into the ditch. Another character, Kirsanov, meets a prostitute and rescues her from her condition with his love (he is a medical student, just like Lisa's admirer). The parodic intention is never acknowledged as such in the text. On the other hand, the underground man himself is always aware that he is behaving (or wants to behave) like the Romantic characters from the early part of the century. Various works and protagonists are mentioned in this context: Gogol (*Dead Souls, Diary of a Madman,* and, by allusion, *The Overcoat*), Goncharov (*A Common Story*), Nekrasov, Byron (*Manfred*), Pushkin (*The Shot*), Lermontov (*Masquerade*), George Sand, even Dostoevsky himself indirectly (*The Insulted and the Injured*). In other words, the liberal literature of the thirties and forties is mocked within situations borrowed from the more radical writers of the sixties, in such a way as to constitute an indirect indictment of both groups.

In contradistinction to Part One, the main role is played in Part Two by liberal and Romantic literature. The narrator-hero is an admirer of Romantic literature and would like to model his behavior on it. However – and here is where parody comes in – this behavior is in reality dictated by a totally different logic, which ensures the failure of the Romantic projects one after another. The contrast is quite striking, for the narrator is not content with vague and nebulous dreams; he imagines each scene to come in detail, sometimes several times in succession, and his predictions are always wrong. Let us take the case of the officer, first of all: he dreams (and we shall see in what respect the dream is Romantic) of a quarrel at the end of which he himself will be thrown out the window ("I would have given anything at that moment for a real, a more regular, a more decent, and a more, so to speak, *literary* quarrel!" [*Notes from the Underground,* 154]); in fact he is treated like someone who is unworthy of a quarrel, someone who does not even exist. Then, in connection with the same officer, he dreams of a reconciliation in love; but he only manages to bump into him – literally – "on the same social footing as he" (161). In the episode with Zverkov, he dreams of a party where everyone admires and loves him; the actual experience is intensely humiliating. With Lisa, finally, he cloaks himself in the most traditionally Romantic dream: "For instance, 'I'm saving Lisa just because she's coming regularly to see me and I'm talking to her. . . . I'm educating her, enlarging her mind. At last I notice that she is in love with me. I pretend not to understand,' " and so on (220). However, when Lisa arrives at his place, he treats her like a prostitute.

His dreams are even more Romantic when they are not followed by any specific action, as in the atemporal dream found in chapter 2: "For instance, I triumphed over everything; all of course lay in the dust at my feet, compelled of their own free will to acknowledge all my perfections, and I forgave them all. I was a famous poet and court chamberlain, and I fell in love; I became a multi-millionaire and at once devoted all my wealth to the improvement of the human race, and there and then confessed all my hideous and shameful crimes before all the people; needless to say, my crimes were, of course, not really hideous or shameful, but had much in them that was 'sublime and beautiful,' something in the style of Manfred" (163), and so forth. Or, in the Zverkov episode, when he anticipates three successive versions of a scene that will never take place. In the first, Zverkov kisses his feet; in the second, they fight a duel; in the third, the narrator bites Zverkov's hand, is sent to prison, and comes back fifteen years later to see his enemy: " 'Look, monster, look at my hollow cheeks and my rags! I've lost everything – my career, my happiness, art, science, *the woman I loved,* and all through you. Here are the pistols. I've come to discharge my pistol and – and I forgive you!' And then I shall fire into the air, and he won't hear of me again. . . . I almost broke into tears, though I knew very well at that moment that the whole thing was *Silvio* and from Lermontov's *Masquarade*" (191–2).

All these dreams occur thus explicitly in the name of literature, a particular form of literature. When events threaten to turn out otherwise, the narrator calls them unliterary ("how paltry, *unliterary,* and commonplace the whole affair would be" [176]). Thus two logics, two conceptions of life take shape: literary or bookish life, and reality, or real life. "We have all lost touch with life, we are all cripples, every one of us – more or less. We have lost touch so much that occasionally we cannot help feeling a sort of disgust with 'real life,' and that is why we are so angry when people remind us of it. Why, we have gone so far that we look upon 'real life' almost as a sort of burden, and we are all agreed that 'life' as we find it in books is much better. . . . Leave us alone without any books, and we shall at once get confused, lose ourselves . . . " (239–40). Thus speaks the disillusioned narrator at the end of *Notes from the Underground.*

Master and Slave

What we have here is not just a rejection of daydreams. The events represented are not organized solely so as to refute the Romantic conception of man, but in terms of their own internal logic. This logic, never formulated but endlessly represented, explains all the apparently aberrant actions of the narrator and the people around him: it is the logic of master and slave, or, as Dostoevsky says, of "scorn" and "humiliation." Far from being the illustration of capriciousness, irrationality, and spontaneity, the behavior of the underground man obeys a very precise schema, as René Girard has already pointed out.

The underground man lives in a world with three levels: inferior, equal, superior. However, these values form a homogeneous series only on the surface. In the first place, the term "equal" can only exist when it is negated: the distinguishing feature of the master–slave relation is its exclusivity, its rejection of any third term. He who aspires to equality proves by that very fact that he does not possess it; he thus finds himself cast in the role of slave. As soon as one person occupies one pole of the relationship, his partner is automatically relegated to the other.

But being a master, is no easier than being a slave. In fact, as soon as one finds one's own superiority confirmed, the superiority disappears by that very token: for superiority exists, paradoxically, only on condition that it be exercised with respect to equals. If one truly believes that the slave is inferior, superiority has no meaning. More precisely, superiority loses its meaning when the master perceives not only his relation to the slave but also the image of that relation; or, to put it another way, when he becomes *conscious* of it. This is precisely where we find the difference between the narrator and the other characters in *Notes from the Underground*. This difference may appear illusory at first glance. The narrator himself believes in it at the age of twenty-four: "Another thing that used to worry me very much at that time was the quite incontestable fact that I was unlike anyone and that there was no one like me. 'I am one, and they are *all,*' I thought – and fell into a melancholy muse" (149). But the narrator adds, sixteen years later: "From all that it can be seen that I was still a very young man" (ibid.). In fact, the difference exists solely in his own eyes; but that is enough. What makes him different from the others is the desire not to be different from them; in other words, his own consciousness, that very consciousness that he had exalted in Part One. As soon as one becomes conscious of the problem of equality, as soon as one declares that one wishes to become equal, one is declaring – in this world where only masters and slaves exist – that one is not equal, and thus – since only masters are "equal" – that one is inferior. Failure stalks the underground man at every turn: equality is impossible; superiority is devoid of meaning; inferiority is painful.

Let us take the first episode, the meeting with the officer. The narrator's desire to see himself thrown out the window might be thought odd, or it might be explained away by the "masochism" the narrator mentioned in Part One. The explanation, however, lies elsewhere, and if we judge his desire absurd, it is because we are taking into account only the explicitly posited acts, and not those they presuppose. Now a regulation quarrel *implies* the equality of the participants: only equals fight. (Nietzsche wrote – no doubt this was the psychology lesson he learned from Dostoevsky: "One does not hate as long as one still despises, but only those whom one esteems equal or higher."[8]) Obeying the same master-slave logic, the officer has to accept this proposition: to demand equality implies that one is inferior; the officer will thus behave like a superior. "He took me by the shoulders and, without a word of warning or explanation, silently carried me bodily from where I was standing to another place and passed me by as though he had not even noticed me" (*Notes from the Underground*, 154). And so our hero finds himself in the place of the slave.

Walled up in his bitterness, the underground man begins to dream – not exactly of revenge, but again of the state of equality. He writes the officer a letter (which he will not send) that is intended to get its recipient either to agree to a duel – implying the equality of the adversaries – or else bring him to the point where he would have "come running to me, fallen on my neck, and offered me his friendship. And how wonderful that would have been! Oh, how wonderfully we should have got on together!" (156) – in other words, to the equality of friendship.

Then the narrator discovers the path of vengeance. It consists in not giving way on Nevsky Avenue where both men often walk. Once again, what he is dreaming of is equality. " 'Why do you always have to step aside first?' I asked myself over and over again in a sort of hysterical rage, sometimes waking up at three o'clock in the morning. 'Why always you and not he? There's no law about it, is there? Why can't you arrange it so that each of you should make way for the other, as usually happens when two well-bred men meet in the street. He yields you half of his pavement and you half of yours, and you pass one another with mutual respect' " (158). And when the encounter takes place, the narrator notes: "I had put myself publicly on the same social footing as he" (161). This moreover is what explains the nostalgia he feels now for that unattractive creature ("I wonder how the dear fellow is getting on now" [161]).

The Zverkov incident obeys precisely the same logic. The underground man enters a room where old school friends are reunited. They too behave as if they do not notice him, which awakens in him the obsessive desire to prove he is their equal. Thus, learning that they are preparing to go out drinking in honor of another old comrade (who does not interest him in the slightest otherwise), he asks to participate in their festivities: to be like the others. Countless obstacles arise in his path; nevertheless, he is determined to surmount them and attend the dinner offered in Zverkov's honor. In his dreams, however, the narrator has no illusions: he sees himself either humiliated by Zverkov, or else, in turn, humiliating him. There is only the choice between self-abasement and contempt for others.

[8] *Beyond Good and Evil: Prelude to a Philosophy of the Future*, trans. Walter Kaufmann (New York: Random House, 1966) chapter 4, "Epigrams and Interludes," no. 173, 92.

Zverkov arrives and behaves affably. But here again, the underground man reacts to what is implied, not what is explicit, and this very affability puts him on guard: "So he already considered himself infinitely superior to me in every respect, did he?... But what if, without the least desire to offend me, the fool had really got the preposterous idea into his head that he was im-measurably superior to me and could not look at me but with a patronizing air?" (178).

They are all seated at a round table; but the equality stops there. Zverkov and his friends make allusions to poverty, to the narrator's misfortunes, in short, to his inferiority – for they too obey the master-slave logic, and as soon as someone demands equality, they understand that he is in fact inferior. They cease to take notice of him, despite all his efforts. "It was quite impossible for anyone to abase himself more disgracefully and do it more willingly" (186). Then, on the first possible occasion, he again demands equality (to go to the whorehouse with them); he meets with rejection; new dreams of superiority follow, and so on.

The other role is not wholly denied him, however: he finds creatures weaker than himself in relation to whom he is master. But that brings him no satis-faction, for he cannot be master in the manner of the "man of action." He needs the process of becoming-a-master, not the state of superiority. This mechanism is evoked in abbreviated form in a school memory: "I did have a sort of friend once, but by that time I was already a tyrant at heart: I wanted to exercise complete authority over him, I wanted to implant a contempt for his surroundings in his heart, I demanded that he should break away from these surroundings, scornfully and finally. I frightened him with my passionate friendship. I reduced him to tears, to hysterics. He was a simple and devoted soul, but the moment I felt that he was completely in my power I grew to hate him and drove him from me, as though I only wanted him for the sake of gaining a victory over him, for the sake of exacting his complete submission to me" (174–5). For a conscious master, the slave offers no further interest once he has been reduced to submission.

But it is especially in the Lisa episode that the underground man finds himself at the other pole of the relationship. Lisa is a prostitute, at the bottom of the social scale: that is what allows the underground man for once to follow the dictates of the Romantic logic he cherishes, to be magnanimous and generous. But his victory is of so little moment that he can forget it: the very next day he is wholly preoccupied with his relationship with his masters. "But *obviously* that was not the chief and most important thing. What I had to do now, and that quickly too, was to save my reputation in the eyes of Zverkov and Simonov. That was the chief thing. And so preoccupied was I with the other affair that I forgot all about Lisa that morning" (215–16). He remembers her later only because he fears that when they next meet he will be unable to hang onto the superiority he had achieved. "Last night I seemed – er – a hero to her and – er – now – h'm!" (218). He fears that Lisa too may become *con-temptuous* and that he will be once again *humiliated*. That is why the first question he asks her is " 'Do you despise me, Lisa?' " (229). After a hysterical crisis, he begins to feel that "our parts were now completely changed, that she was the heroine now, while I was exactly the same crushed and humiliated creature as she had appeared to me that night – four days before . . . " (234). This triggers his desire to be master again; he possesses her, then hands her money as if she were a mere prostitute. But the state of mastery does not bring him pleasure, and all he wants is for Lisa to leave. Once she has gone, however, he discovers that she has not taken the money. Thus she is not inferior! She regains her full value in his eyes, and he rushes out after her. "Why? To fall on my knees before her, to sob with remorse, to kiss her feet, to beseech her to forgive me!" (238). Lisa was useless to him as a slave; she becomes necessary again as a potential master.

It is now clearer that the underground man's reveries are not external to the master-slave logic: they are the positive version of what the master's behavior represents negatively. The Romantic relation of equality or generosity presupposes superiority, just as the quarrel presupposes equality. Talking to Lisa about their first meeting, the narrator recognizes this fully: " 'I had been humiliated, so I too wanted to show my power. That's what happened, and you thought I'd come there specially to save you, did you?' " (p. 231). " 'Power was what I wanted then. I wanted sport. I wanted to see you cry. I wanted to humiliate you. To make you hysterical. That's what I wanted' " (ibid.). Not only is Romantic logic defeated at every turn by the master-slave logic, it does not differ from master-slave logic; moreover, that is why "positive" dreams can alternate freely with "negative" ones.

The plot of Part Two of *Notes from the Underground,* taken as a whole, is merely an exploitation of these two basic figures in the master-slave game: the vain attempt to achieve equality, ending in humiliation; and the equally vain effort – for its results are ephemeral – to avenge oneself, which is only, in the best of cases, a compensatory device: one humiliates and despises, in order to have humiliated and despised. The first episode (involving the officer) presents a condensed version of both possibilities. Then the two modes appear in alternation, according to a principle of contrast: the underground man is humiliated by Zverkov and his comrades; he humiliates Lisa; he is again humiliated by his servant Apollon; he takes it out on Lisa. The parallelism of the situations is marked either by the identity of the character or by some resemblance in the details: thus Apollon "always lisped and minced his words" (222), while Zverkov speaks by "mouthing and lisping, which he never used to do before" (p. 178). The episode with Apollon, which dramatizes a concrete relation between master and servant, is emblematic of this set of hardly random incidents.

Being and Otherness

The underground man is continually driven to assume the role of slave. He suffers cruelly from this role, yet he seems to seek it out. Why? Because the logic of the master-slave relation itself is not an ultimate truth, it is a posited appearance concealing an essential presupposition that we now have to uncover. This center, this essence we are approaching holds a surprise in reserve for us, however: it consists in affirming the primordial nature of the relation with the other, in locating the essence of being in the other, in telling us that what is simple is double, and that the ultimate, undivided atom is made up of two. The underground man does not exist apart from his relation with the other, without the other's gaze. And not being is an even more distressing state than being nothing, than being a slave.

Man does not exist without the gaze of the other. The meaning of the gaze in *Notes from the Underground* may be misunderstood, however. In fact, references to it, which are numerous, seem at first glance to be inscribed within the master-slave logic. The narrator does not want to look at the others, for in doing so he would be recognizing their existence and by that very token granting them a privilege that he is not sure he has for himself; in other words, the gaze risks making him a slave. "When at work in the office I tried not to look at anyone . . . " (147). When he meets his old school friends, he insistently avoids their glances, he keeps his eyes fixed on his plate (180); "I just did my best not to look at them . . . " (185). When he looks at someone, he tries to put all his dignity – and thus his defiance – into his gaze. "I stared at him with hatred and malice" (155), he says about the officer; and regarding his school friends, "I looked at them impudently with leaden eyes" (182). Let us recall that the Russian words *prezirat'* and *nenavidt'*, to despise and to hate – terms used quite frequently in the text to describe just this feeling – both contain a root verb meaning to see or to look.

The others behave just the same way, with more success, most of the time. The officer passes by as though he has not seen him (154), Simonov tries not to look at him (170); his friends, once they are drunk, pay no attention to him (182). And when they do look at him, they do so just as aggressively, just as defiantly. Ferfichkin glares furiously at him (181), Trudolyubov throws "a disdainful glance in [his] direction" (183), and Apollon, his servant, specializes in scornful looks: "He started by fixing me with a stern glare which he kept up for several minutes at a time, particularly when he used to meet me or when I went out of the house. . . . He would suddenly and without any excuse whatsoever enter my room quietly and smoothly when I was either reading or pacing my room, and remain standing at the door, with one hand behind his back and one foot thrust forward, and stare fixedly at me. This time his stare was not only stern but witheringly contemptuous. If I suddenly asked him what he wanted, he would not reply, but continue to stare straight at me for a few more seconds, then he would purse his lips with a specially significant expression, turn round slowly, and slowly go back to his room" (223–4).

The rare occasions when the underground man manages to carry out his Romantic fantasies have to be analyzed from the same point of view. Success requires the total absence of any gaze. Not by coincidence, this is the scenario in the underground man's victorious encounter with the officer: "Suddenly, only three paces from my enemy, I quite unexpectedly made up my mind, shut my eyes, and – we knocked violently against each other, shoulder to shoulder" (160). The same scenario is played out, even more predictably, during the first encounter with Lisa. Very early in the conversation, the narrator tells us: "The candle went out. I could no longer make out her face" (196). Only at the very end, after his speechmaking is over, does he find "a box of matches and a candle-stick with a new unused candle" (213). Now it is precisely between these two moments of light that the underground man can make his romantic statements, can show the positive side of the master's face.

But this is merely the logic of the "literal," concrete gaze. In fact, in all these incidents, the underground man accepts the condition of inferiority, even seeks it out, because it allows the gaze of others to be fixed on himself, if only with scorn. The underground man is always mindful of the suffering that the humiliating gaze causes him; he goes after it nonetheless. To go to the home of his boss Anton Antonovich brings him no pleasure; the conversations he hears there are banal. "The usual topic of conversation was excise duties, the hard bargaining in the Senate, salaries, promotions, His Excellency, the best way to please him, etc., etc. I had the patience to sit like a damn fool beside these people for hours, listening to them, neither daring to speak to them, nor knowing what to say. I got more and more bored, broke out into a sweat, and was in danger of getting an apoplectic stroke. But all this was good and useful to me" (165). Why? Because he had previously felt "an irresistible urge to plunge into social life" (164). He knows that Simonov despises him: "I suspected that he really loathed the sight of me . . . I could not help thinking that this particular gentleman must be sick and tired of me and that I was wasting my time going to see him" (166). But he goes on to explain that "such reflections merely spurred me on to put myself into an equivocal position" (ibid.). A gaze, even a master's gaze, is better than the absence of any gaze.

The entire scene with Zverkov and the schoolmates can be explained in the same way. The underground man needs their gaze; if he puts on distant airs, it is because he is waiting patiently "for them to speak to [him] first" (185). Subsequently, "I did my best to show them that I could do without them, at the same time deliberately stamping on the floor, raising myself up and down on my heels" (186). It is the same story with Apollon: he gets no use out of this crude and lazy servant, but he cannot let go of him either. "I could not get rid of him, as though he formed one chemical substance with me. . . . For some confounded reason Apollon seemed to be an integral part of my flat, and for seven years I could not get rid of him" (222–3). Here is the explanation of the irrational "masochism" reported by the narrator in Part One and relished by the critics. The underground man accepts suffering because the condition of a slave is finally the only one that assures him of the gaze of others; without that gaze, the human being does not exist.

In fact, Part One already explicitly contained that assertion, made on the basis of a postulate of failure: the underground man is precisely nothing, not even a slave, or, as he says, not even an insect. "Not only did I not become spiteful, I did not even know how to become anything, either spiteful or good, either a blackguard or an honest man, either a hero or an insect" (109). He dreams of being able to assert himself, if only through negative traits such as laziness, the absence of actions and good points. "I should have respected myself just because I should at least have been able to be lazy; I should at least have possessed one quality which might be mistaken for a positive one and in which I could have believed myself. Question – who is he? Answer – a loafer. I must say it would have been a real pleasure to have heard that said about myself, for it would have meant that a positive definition had been found for me and that there was something one could say about me" (124). For now he cannot even say that he is nothing (and get around the negation in the attribute); he *is not,* and the very verb of existence itself turns out to be denied. To be alone is no longer to be.

A great quasi-scientific debate occupies almost all the pages of *Notes from the Underground,* having to do with the very conception of man and his psychic structure. The underground man is seeking to prove that the conception opposed to his is not only amoral (it is amoral in a secondary, derivative way) but also inexact, false. The man of nature and truth, the simple and immediate man, imagined by Rousseau, is not only inferior to the conscious underground man; he does not even exist. Unified, simple, and indivisible man is a fiction. The very simplest is already dual; the human being has no existence prior to the other or independent of him. That indeed is why the dreams of "rational egoism" cherished by Chernyshevsky and his friends are condemned to failure, as is every theory that is not based upon the duality of being. This universality of the conclusions is asserted in the closing pages of *Notes:* "I have merely carried to extremes in my life what you have not dared to carry even halfway, and, in addition, you have mistaken your cowardice for common sense and have found comfort in that, deceiving yourselves" (240).

Thus in one and the same stroke the narrator rejects an essentialist conception of man and an objective vision of ideas; it is no accident that allusions to Rousseau are scattered throughout the text. Rousseau's confession was written *for others* but by an *autonomous* being; that of the underground man is written *for himself,* but he himself is already *double,* the others are in him, the outside is inside. Just as it is impossible to conceive of man as simple and autonomous, we have to transcend the idea of the autonomous text seen as an authentic expression of a subject, rather than as a reflection of other texts, as play among interlocutors. These are not two different problems, the one having to do with the nature of man, the other with language, one located among "ideas," the other in "form." We are talking about one and the same thing.

The Symbolic Game

Thus the apparently chaotic and contradictory aspects of *Notes from the Underground* turn out to be coherent. The moral masochism, the master-slave logic, the new status of the idea are all part of a single underlying structure, which is semiotic rather than psychic: the structure of alterity. Of all the essential elements singled out during our analysis, there remains just one whose place in the whole has not become apparent: the denunciations of the powers of reason, in Part One. Might these be a gratuitous attack on Dostoevsky's part against his enemy-friends the Socialists? But as we finish reading the text, we shall discover their place too, and their meaning.

In fact, I have left aside one of the most important characters in Part Two: Lisa. I have done so deliberately, for her behavior does not obey any of the mechanisms described up to now. For example, let us observe her gaze: it resembles neither the master's nor the slave's. "I caught sight of a fresh, young, somewhat pale face, with straight dark eyebrows, and with a serious, as it were, surprised look in her eyes" (193). "Suddenly, close beside me, I saw two wide-open eyes observing me intently and curiously. The look in those eyes was coldly indifferent and sullen, as though it were utterly detached, and it made me feel terribly depressed" (194–5). At the end of their meeting: "It was altogether a different face, altogether a different look from a few hours ago – sullen, mistrustful, and obstinate. Now her eyes were soft and beseeching, and at the same time trustful, tender, and shy. So do children look at people they are very fond of and from whom they expect some favour. She had light-brown eyes, beautiful and full of life, eyes which could express love as well as sullen hatred" (213–14). At his place, after having witnessed a painful scene, her gaze retains its uniqueness: "she regarded me uneasily" (228); "she glanced at me a few times in mournful perplexity" (230); and so on.

The crucial moment in the story recounted in *Notes from the Underground* comes when Lisa, insulted by the narrator, reacts abruptly and in an unexpected manner, a manner that does not belong to the master-slave logic. The surprise is such that the narrator himself has to emphasize it: "But here a very odd thing happened. I was so used to imagining everything and to thinking of everything as it happened in books, and to picturing to myself everything in the world as I had previously made it up in my dreams, that at first I could not all at once grasp the meaning of this occurrence. What occurred was this: Lisa, humiliated and crushed by me, understood much more than I imagined" (233).

How does she react? "She suddenly jumped up from her chair with a kind of irresistible impulse and, all drawn towards me but still feeling very shy and not daring to move from her place, held out her hands to me. . . . It was here that my heart failed me. Then she rushed to me flung her arms round my neck, and burst into tears" (233). Lisa rejects both the master's role and the slave's; she does not wish to dominate or to take pleasure in her own suffering; she loves the other *for himself*. It is this outburst of light that makes *Notes* a much clearer work than it is usually considered to be; it is this very scene that allows the narrative to come to a close. While on the surface the narrative is presented as a fragment chopped off through the whim of fate, in fact the book could not have ended earlier, and there is no reason for it to go further; as "Dostoevsky" says in the closing line, "we may stop here" (240). Now we understand, too, something that has often troubled Dostoevsky's commentators. We know from one of the author's letters, contemporary with the book, that the original manuscript introduced a positive principle at the end of Part One: the narrator indicated that the answer lay in Christ. The censors suppressed this passage in the first edition of the book; curiously, Dostoevsky never reinserted it in later editions. The reason for this now becomes clear. The book would have had two endings instead of one, and Dostoevsky's point would have lost much of its force had it been placed in the narrator's mouth rather than in Lisa's action.

Several critics (Skaftymov, Frank) have already remarked that, contrary to popular opinion, Dostoevsky does not defend the underground man's views but rather contests them. The misunderstanding may arise because we are dealing with two simultaneous dialogues. First, there is the dialogue between the underground man and the defender of rational egoism (it hardly matters whether we attach to it Chernyshevsky's name, or Rousseau's, or someone else's). This debate bears upon the nature of man, and it contrasts two images, the one autonomous, the other dual; it is obvious that Dostoevsky accepts the second one as true. But this first dialogue only serves to sweep away the misunderstanding that obscured the real debate; here is where the second dialogue comes in, this time between the underground man on the one hand and Lisa, or, alternatively, "Dostoevsky," on the other. The major difficulty in interpreting *Notes from the Underground* lies in the impossibility of reconciling the arguments of the underground man, presented as true, with Dostoevsky's position as we know it from other sources. But this difficulty arises from the telescoping of the two debates into one. The underground man is not the representative of the moral position, inscribed by Dostoevsky into the text in his own name; he simply carries to its extreme consequences the position of Dostoevsky's adversaries, the radicals of the 1860s. But once these positions have been logically presented, the essential debate unfolds, even though it occupies only a part of the text. In this debate Dostoevsky, while placing himself in the framework of alterity, contrasts the master-slave logic with that of the love of others for their own sake, as this logic is embodied in Lisa's behavior. If in the first debate we find two descriptions of man that are opposed on the level of *truth,* in the second, where the solution to this problem is taken for granted, the author opposes two conceptions of proper behavior on the *moral* plane.

In *Notes from the Underground,* the second solution appears only for a brief moment, when Lisa abruptly holds out her arms to embrace the man who is insulting her. But starting with this book, the solution is asserted more and more forcefully in Dostoevsky's work, even though it remains as the mark of a limit rather than becoming the central theme of a narrative. In *Crime and Punishment,* the prostitute Sonia listens to Raskolnikov's confessions with the same love as Lisa. Prince Myshkin in *The Idiot* behaves the same way; so does Tikhon, who hears Stavrogin's confession in *The Demons.* And in *The Brothers Karamazov,* the same gesture is repeated, symbolically, three times: at the very beginning of the book, the *starets* Zossima approaches the great sinner Mitia and bows silently before him to the ground. Christ, who hears the speech of the Grand Inquisitor threatening him with burning at the stake, approaches the old man and silently kisses his bloodless lips. And Aliosha, after hearing Ivan's "revolt," finds in himself the same response: he approaches Ivan and kisses him on the mouth without saying a word. This gesture, varied and repeated throughout Dostoevsky's work, takes on a specific value. The wordless embrace, the silent kiss transcend language without renouncing meaning. Verbal language, self-consciousness, the master-slave logic, all three turn out to be on the same side; they remain the hallmarks of the underground man. For language, as we were told in the first part of *Notes from the Underground*, knows only the linguistic, just as reason knows only the reasonable – that is, a twentieth part of what constitutes a human being. The mouth that no longer *speaks* but *embraces* introduces the gesture and the body (according to the narrator of *Notes from the Underground* we have all lost our "proper body"); it interrupts language but inaugurates the symbolic circuit all the more forcefully. Language will be surpassed not by the haughty silence incarnated by "the man of nature and of truth," the man of action, but by this higher symbolic game that governs Lisa's pure act.

The day after the death of his first wife, during precisely the period when he was working on *Notes from the Underground*, Dostoevsky wrote in his notebook: "To love a person *as one's own self* according to the commandment of Christ is impossible. The law of individuality is the constraint, 'I' is the stumbling block . . . Meanwhile, after the appearance of Christ as *the idea of man incarnate*, it became as clear as day that the highest, final development of the individual should attain precisely the point (at the very end of his development, at the very point of reaching the goal), where man might find, recognize, and with all the strength of his nature be convinced that the highest use which he can make of his individuality, of the full development of his *I*, is to seemingly annihilate that *I* to give it wholly to each and everyone wholeheartedly and selflessly. And this is the greatest happiness."[9]

This time, I think, we may let the author have the last word.

[9] *The Unpublished Dostoevsky, Diaries and Notebooks (1860–81)*, ed. Carl R. Proffer (Ann Arbor: Ardis, 1973) vol. 1, 39 (April 16, 1864).

8 *The Limits of Edgar Poe*

Anyone encountering Edgar Allan Poe's tales for the first time cannot help being struck by their tremendous variety.[1] Alongside the well-known fantastic tales like "The Black Cat" or "Metzengerstein," one finds stories like "The Gold-Bug" or "The Purloined Letter" his "tales of ratiocination." There are tales that prefigure the "horror story" – "Hop-Frog," "The Masque of the Red Death" – and others that belong to the "grotesque" (to borrow the vocabulary of the period): "King Pest," "The Devil in the Belfry," "Lionizing". Poe excelled in pure adventure narratives ("The Pit and the Pendulum," "A Descent into the Maelström") as well as in static descriptive tales ("The Island of the Fay," "The Domain of Arnheim"). As if this were not enough, he also wrote philosophical dialogues ("The Power of Words," "The Colloquy of Monos and Una") and allegorical tales ("The Oval Portrait," "William Wilson"). Some readers see his work as the origin of the detective story ("The Murders in the Rue Morgue") or of science fiction ("The Unparalleled Adventure of One Hans Pfaall"). All in all, the reader bent on classification is bound to be disconcerted.

This striking variety of scope is accompanied by another form of diversity that may manifest itself within a single tale. Poe has benefited – and continues to benefit – from the attention of critics who have seen in his work the most perfect illustration of a certain ideal – which turns out however to be a different ideal in each case. In his preface in the second group of stories he translated (*Nouvelles Histoires extraordinaires*), Baudelaire offers Poe as the example of the decadent spirit, the model for partisans of Art for Art's sake to follow: Baudelaire sees in Poe what interests him personally.[2] For Valéry, Poe perfectly embodied the tendency that consists in mastering the creative process, reducing

---

[1] *The Complete Tales and Poems of Edgar Allan Poe,* intr. Hervey Allen (New York: Modern Library [Random House], 1938). All page references to Poe's stories are to this edition.

[2] Preface to *Nouvelles histoires extraordinaires,* in *Baudelaire on Poe,* trans. and ed. Lois and Francis E. Hyslop, Jr. (State College, PA: Bald Eagle Press, 1951) 119–44.

it to a set of rules instead of letting blind inspiration take all the initiatives.[3] Marie Bonaparte took Poe as the subject of one of the most famous (and most controversial) essays in psychoanalytical criticism: according to her, his work illustrates all the major psychic complexes that had recently been described.[4] Bachelard read Poe as a master of material imagination;[5] Jean Ricardou read him as a skilled practitioner of anagrams;[6] and so on. Are all these critics really discussing the same author? How can the same works serve as the example – and even the privileged example – of such widely divergent critical tendencies?

As with any author, then, but in a particularly striking way here, Poe's work poses a challenge for the commentator. Is there a single generative principle common to such diverse writings? Do Poe's tales trace that "figure in the carpet" whose parable Henry James formulated? Let us attempt to clarify the issue, even if we have to abandon some certainties to do so.

Just such a generative principle was identified by Poe's first great admirers (and if the value of a poet were to be measured by that of his admirers, Poe would be one of the greatest): Baudelaire and Dostoevsky. But they both failed to appreciate its full importance, or so it seems, for they perceived it in one of its concrete realizations and not as a fundamental movement. Baudelaire had the right word, "exception," but when he spoke of "the exceptional case" he hastened to add "in the moral order"; he asserted that "no one . . . has told about the *exceptions* in human life and nature with more magic . . ." but he was content to continue by listing a few thematic elements.[7] Similarly, Dostoevsky asserted that Poe "almost always chooses the rarest reality and places his hero in the most unaccustomed circumstance or psychological situation."[8]

Now rather than possessing a thematic common denominator, these tales all stem from an abstract principle that engenders what is called "technique," "style," or "narrative" as well as "ideas." Poe is the author of the extreme, the excessive, the superlative; he pushes everything to its limits – and beyond, where possible. He is interested only in the greatest or the smallest: the point where a quality achieves its highest degree, or else (but this often amounts to the same thing) where it threatens to turn itself into its opposite. This single principle determines the most varied aspects of his work. Baudelaire summed it up best, perhaps, in the title he devised for the first collection he published; "Histoires *extraordinaires.*"

Let us begin with the most obvious starting point, Poe's themes. We have

---

[3] Paul Valéry, *Oeuvres I* (Paris: Editions de la Pléiade [Gallimard] 1957).

[4] Marie Bonaparte, *The Life and Works of Edgar Allan Poe: A Psycho-Analytic Introduction,* trans. John Rodker (London: Imago, 1949).

[5] Gaston Bachelard, *L'Eau et les rêves* (Paris: José Corti, 1942).

[6] Jean Ricardou, *Problèmes du Nouveau Roman* (Paris, Editions du Seuil, 1967).

[7] Preface to *Histoires extraordinaires,* in *Baudelaire on Poe,* pp. 115–16.

[8] Dostoevsky's discussion of three of Poe's tales appeared in *Vremja* in January, 1861. The citation is taken from the French translation published as: Féodor Dostoevsky, *Récits, chroniques et polémiques* (Paris: Gallimard, 1969) 1091–2.

already mentioned the inclusion of some fantastic tales, but the fantastic is nothing but a prolonged hesitation between a natural explanation of events and a supernatural one. It amounts to playing with the boundary between the natural and the supernatural. Poe says so quite explicitly in the first lines of his fantastic stories, by stating the alternative: the explanation is either madness (or dreaming) – and therefore natural – or else supernatural intervention. Thus, in "The Black Cat": "Mad indeed would I be to expect it [belief on the part of his readers], in a case where my very senses reject their own evidence. Yet, mad am I not – and very surely do I not dream. . . . Hereafter, perhaps, some intellect may be found which will reduce my phantasm to the commonplace – some intellect more calm, more logical, and far less excitable than my own, which will perceive, in the circumstances I detail with awe, nothing more than an ordinary succession of very natural causes and effects" (223). Or in "The Tell-Tale Heart": "True! – Nervous – very, very dreadfully nervous I had been and am; but why *will* you say that I am mad?" (303).

The tone of these explorations of limits is not always so solemn; the hesitation between human and animal takes place in a humorous vein in "Four Beasts in One," the tale of a camelopard king, or, at this same boundary between madness and reason, in "The System of Doctor Tarr and Professor Fether." But, on the thematic plane, one limit attracts Poe more than any other, and this is perfectly understandable since it is the limit par excellence, that of death. Death haunts nearly every page of Poe's work.

The obsession, allied to the most diverse points of view, illuminates quite varied aspects of non-life. As one might expect, murder plays a primary role; and it appears in all its forms: via a sharp knife ("The Black Cat"), suffocation ("The Tell-Tale Heart"), poison ("The Imp of the Perverse"), walling in ("The Cask of Amontillado"), fire ("Hop-Frog"), or water ("The Mystery of Marie Rogêt"). The fatality of "natural" death is also a recurring theme, whether such death is collective ("The Masque of the Red Death," "Shadow – A Parable") or individual ("A Tale of the Ragged Mountains"); there is also the threat of imminent death ("The Pit and the Pendulum," "A Descent into the Maelström"). Poe's allegories often deal with death ("The Island of the Fay," "The Oval Portrait") and his philosophical dialogues have as their theme life after death, as in "The Colloquy of Monos and Una," or "The Conversation of Eiros and Charmion." The theme of life after death brings to light with exceptional clarity the limit separating the two. And Poe makes numerous excursions into this domain: survival of a mummy ("Some Words with a Mummy"), survival through magnetism ("The Facts in the Case of M. Valdemar"), resurrection through love ("Morella," "Ligeia," "Eleonora").

One other facet of death particularly fascinates Poe: the burial of a living being. The burial may be caused by the desire to kill ("The Cask of Amontillado") or to hide the corpse ("The Tell-Tale Heart," "The Black Cat"). In the most striking case, the burial takes place by mistake: a living person is buried because he or she is taken for dead. This is the case with Berenice and Madeline Usher. Poe describes the cataleptic states that bring about this confusion: "Among the numerous train of maladies superinduced by that fatal and primary one which effected a revolution of so horrible a kind in the moral and physical being of my cousin, may be mentioned as the most distressing and obstinate in its nature, a species of epilepsy not unfrequently terminating in *trance* itself – trance very nearly resembling positive dissolution, and from which her manner of recovery was, in most instances, startlingly abrupt" ("Berenice," 643). Trances raise the play with limits to a higher power: not only death in life (as with every death) but life in death. If burial is the path of death, premature burial is a negation of a negation.

It must be understood, however, that this fascination with death is not the direct result of some morbid impulse; it is the product of an overall tendency which is the systematic exploration of limits to which Poe devotes himself (an exploration that might be called his "superlativism"). The proof of the greater generality of this generative principle is that its effects may be observed on much less macabre phenomena. This is true almost at the level of the grammatical characteristics of Poe's style, which is rich in superlatives. The reader encounters them on every page; let us cite a few, at random: "It is impossible that any deed could have been wrought with a more thorough deliberation" ("The Imp of the Perverse," 283). "To the uttermost regions of the globe have not the indignant winds bruited its unparalleled infamy?" ("William Wilson," 626). "The school-room was the largest in the house – I could not help thinking, in the world" ("William Wilson," 628). "Yet there are no towers in the land more time-honored than my gloomy, gray, hereditary halls" ("Berenice," 642). "Surely, man had never before so terribly altered, in so brief a period, as had Roderick Usher" (134). "Oh! most unrelenting! oh! most demoniac of men!" ("The Pit and the Pendulum," 256). ". . . a wailing shriek, half of horror and half of triumph, such as might have arisen only out of hell" ("The Black Cat," 230). "A fearful idea now suddenly drove the blood in torrents upon my heart . . . " ("The Pit and the Pendulum," 248).

Superlatives, hyperbole, antithesis: such are the weapons of this somewhat facile rhetoric. This is no doubt the most dated aspect of Poe's work for contemporary readers, accustomed as they are to more discreet descriptions. Poe consumes so many excessive feelings in his sentences that he leaves none for the reader; the word "terror" leaves us cold (whereas we would be terrorized by an evocation that does not name it but simply suggests it). When he exclaims, for example, "oh, mournful and terrible engine of Horror and of Crime – of Agony and of Death!" ("The Black Cat," 227), the narrator deploys so much emotion that his partner, the reader, does not know what to do with his own. But it would undoubtedly be a mistake to stop at this observation of Poe's "bad taste" – as it would to see in his work the immediate (and precious) expression of morbid fantasies. Poe's superlatives stem from the same generative principle as his fascination with death.

The consequences of this principle have not yet all been spelled out. For Poe is sensitive to all limits – including the one that gives his own writings the status of literature, of fiction. We know him as the author of numerous essays (some of which were translated by Baudelaire); but alongside these, there are countless texts of uncertain status that his editors have hesitated to include in one category or another. "Mesmeric Revelation" is sometimes classified among the essays, sometimes among the "stories"; so is "Maelzel's Chess-Player." Texts such as "Silence – A Fable," "Shadow – A Parable," "The Power of Words," "The Colloquy of Monos and Una," "The Conversation of Eiros and Charmion" retain only weak traces (though the traces are unmistakable) of their fictional status. The most striking case is that of "The Imp of the Perverse," to which Baudelaire gave first place in *Nouvelles Histoires extraordinaires*. During the first two-thirds of the text we seem to be dealing with a "theoretical study," an exposition of Poe's ideas; then suddenly the narrative comes to the fore, profoundly transforming all that precedes, leading us to correct our initial reaction: the imminence of death gives a new sheen to the cold reflections that have gone before. The limit between fiction and nonfiction is thus illuminated – and pulverized.

These are still surface features of Poe's work, features susceptible to immediate observation. But the principle of limits determines the work more basically, through a fundamental aesthetic choice which every writer confronts and in the face of which Poe opts once again for an extreme solution. A classical work of fiction is at one and the same time, and necessarily, an imitation – that is, a relation with the world and with memory – and a game, which entails rules; and an organization of its own elements. Some element of the work – a scene, a decor, a character – is always the result of a dual determination, one stemming from the other elements that are copresent in the text, the other imposed by "verisimilitude," "realism," our knowledge of the world. The equilibrium that is established between these two types of factors may vary greatly, depending on whether one moves from the "formalists" to the "naturalists." But the disproportion between the factors rarely reaches so high a degree as in Poe. Here, nothing is imitation, everything is construction and game.

It would be fruitless to search in Poe's tales for a picture of American life in the first half of the nineteenth century. The action typically takes place in old manor houses, macabre castles, distant and unknown lands. Poe's decor is completely conventional: it is whatever the plot requires. There is a pond near the house of Usher so that the house can cave in, not because the region is known for its ponds. We have seen that his narratives are well endowed not only with superlative expressions but also with superlative characters: they are the inhabitants of Poe's tales, not of Poe's America. The few exceptions to this rule only confirm it. The description of the school, in "William Wilson," may be based on Poe's personal experience in England; the woman who comes back to life, Ligeia or Eleonora, may evoke his wife, who died young. But what a distance there is between the real experience and these excessive actions and supernatural characters! Baudelaire himself, succumbing to the realist and expressive illusion, believed that Poe had traveled widely; it was in fact Poe's brother who traveled, and

Edgar who told the stories. Poe is an adventurer, but not in the ordinary sense of the term; he explores the possibilities of the mind, the mysteries of artistic creation, the secrets of the blank page.

He discussed this himself at length, moreover, in texts on art and literature such as "The Philosophy of Composition," translated by Baudelaire as "la Genèse d'un poème" (Baudelaire had some doubts as to Poe's sincerity, however). Poe recounts the production of his well-known poem, "The Raven": not one line, not one word can be attributed to chance (that means, as well, to any relation with the "real"): each one is there on the strength of its relation to other words, other lines (I have already had occasion to invoke this text). "I made the night tempestuous, first, to account for the Raven's seeking admission, and secondly, for the effect of contrast with the (physical) serenity within the chamber. I made the bird alight on the bust of Pallas, also for the effect of contrast between the marble and the plumage – it being understood that the bust was absolutely *suggested* by the bird – the bust of Pallas being chosen, first, as most in keeping with the scholarship of the love, and, secondly, for the sonorousness of the word, Pallas, itself."[9] Elsewhere he openly avows his distaste for the principle of imitation: "All other arts... have... advanced at a far greater rate – each very nearly in the direct ratio of its non-imitativeness,"[10] and also: "The mere imitation, however accurate, of what is in Nature, entitles no man to the sacred name of 'Artist.' "[11]

Poe is thus not a "painter of life," but a builder, an inventor of forms; this accounts for the exploration mentioned earlier of the most varied genres (if not their invention). The arrangement of the elements of a tale matters much more to him than their harmonization with what we know of the world. Once again Poe reaches a limit: that of the suppression of imitation, of the exceptional valorization of construction.

This fundamental choice has numerous consequences, which figure among the most characteristic features of Poe's writings. Let us list some of them.

First of all, Poe's tales (like his other works) are always very rigorously constructed. In his theory of the short story (developed in a review of Hawthorne's tales), Poe had already articulated this necessity: "A skilful literary artist has constructed a tale. If wise, he has not fashioned his thoughts to accommodate his incidents; but having conceived, with deliberate care, a certain unique or single *effect* to be wrought out, he then invents such incidents – he then combines such events as may best aid him in establishing this preconceived effect. If his very initial sentence tend not to the outbringing of this effect, then he has failed in his first step. In the whole composition there should

⁹ Edgar Allan Poe, "The Philosophy of Composition," in *Literary Criticism of Edgar Allan Poe,* ed. Robert L. Hough (Lincoln: University of Nebraska Press, 1965) 29.
¹⁰ Edgar Allan Poe, "Marginalia," in *The Brevities,* ed. Burton R. Pollin (New York: Gordian Press, 1985) no. 131, 232.
¹¹ Edgar Allan Poe, "Marginalia," no. 242, 385.

be no word written, of which the tendency, direct or indirect, is not to the one pre-established design."[12]

In the passage quoted earlier from "The Philosophy of Composition," two types of internal constraints are identifiable. One stems from causality, from logical coherence, the other from symmetry, from contrast and gradation, thus giving the work a coherence that could be called spatial. The rigor of causality leads to tales that are constructed in the spirit of the deductive method Poe cherished, such as "The Gold-Bug," "The Purloined Letter," or "The Murders in the Rue Morgue." But it also has less immediate consequences; and one may wonder whether Poe's discovery of the "imp of the perverse" does not have something to do with this. This particular state of mind consists in acting "for the reason that we ought not to do it"; but rather than stopping at such a negative observation, Poe constructs a faculty of the human spirit whose property is to determine such acts. Thus the gesture that is the most absurd in appearance is not left unexplained, it too participates in the general determinism (along the way, Poe discovers the role of certain unconscious motivations). In a more general way, we might be inclined to think that the fantastic genre attracts Poe precisely because of his rationalism (and not in spite of it). If one limits oneself to natural explanations, one must accept chance, coincidences in the organization of life; if one wants everything to be determined, one must also recognize supernatural causes. Dostoevsky declared the same thing about Poe – after his own fashion: "If he is fantastic, it is only superficially."[13] Poe is fantastic because he is superrational, not because he is irrational, and there is no contradiction between the fantastic tales and the tales of ratiocination.

Poe's causal rigor is paralleled by a formal spatial rigor. Gradation is the informing principle of many of the tales: Poe first captures the reader's attention by a general announcement of the extraordinary events that he wishes to relate; next he presents the entire background of the action in great detail; then the rhythm accelerates, often ending in a concluding statement charged with the greatest meaning which at once clears up the mystery that has been carefully maintained and announces some fact, generally horrible. Thus the last sentence of "The Black Cat": "I had walled the monster up within the tomb" (230).

This formal determinism operates on several levels. One of the most eloquent is that of sound, for many of the tales function on the level of word play: in particular, several of the grotesque tales, such as "Lionizing," "King Pest," "Some Words with a Mummy" (the hero of this last story is called Allamistakeo). But the same thing is true of other tales where the formal determinations are less apparent; Jean Ricardou has demonstrated the role played by certain verbal correspondences in stories like "The Gold-Bug" or "A Tale of the Ragged Mountains." Finally, the technique of embedding, in

[12] Edgar Allan Poe, "Hawthorne's *Twice-Told Tales*," in *Literary Criticism of Edgar Allan Poe*, 136.
[13] *Récits, chroniques et polémiques*, 1091.

which the tale related within another one is in every respect similar to the first, is frequent in Poe, and it is particularly apparent in "The Fall of the House of Usher," where the framing narrative imitates both a painting and a book to which it introduces us.

Each level of textual organization obeys a rigorous logic; furthermore, these levels are strictly coordinated among themselves. To take just one example: the fantastic and "serious" tales are always recounted in the first person, preferably by the main character, with no distance between the narrator and his tale (the circumstances of the narration play an important role here). This is the case in "The Imp of the Perverse," "The Black Cat," "William Wilson," "The Tell-Tale Heart," "Berenice," and so on. On the other hand, the "grotesque" tales such as "King Pest," "The Devil in the Belfry," "Lionizing," "Four Beasts in One," "Some Words with a Mummy," or the horror stories like "Hop-Frog" and "The Masque of the Red Death" are related in the third person or by a narrator who is a witness, not a participant; the events are distanced, the tone stylized. No straddling is possible.

A second consequence of the extreme choice made by Poe (against imitation, in favor of construction) is the disappearance of narrative, or at least of its simple and basic form. One might find such an assertion surprising, given that Poe is often judged a narrator par excellence; but an attentive reading will convince us that one almost never finds in his writing a straightforward linking of consecutive events. Even in the adventure stories that come the closest, such as "MS. Found in a Bottle" or "Narrative of A. Gordon Pym," the story, which begins as a simple series of adventures, turns into a mystery, and compels us to turn back on it, to reread its enigmas more attentively. The same is true of the tales of ratiocination which, in this respect, are very far from contemporary forms of the detective novel: the logic of the action is replaced by that of the search for knowledge, so that we never witness the linking of causes and effects, only their deduction after the fact.

Thus traditional narrative is absent, and so too is ordinary psychology as a means of construction of the story. The determinism of facts takes the place of psychological motivation, as has often been noted, and Poe's characters, victims of a causality that surpasses them, always lack depth. Poe is incapable of constructing a true alterity: the monologue is his preferred style, and even his dialogues ("Colloquy," "Conversation") are disguised monologues. Psychology arouses his interest only as a problem among others, a mystery to unravel; as an object, not a method of construction. The proof is found in a tale like "The Purloined Letter," in which Dupin, a puppet-character lacking in all "psychology" in the novelistic sense, offers lucid formulations of the laws of human psychic life.

Narrative is by its nature imitative, repeating in the succession of events it evokes that of the pages turned by the reader; Poe will thus find ways of getting rid of it. And first of all the most obvious way: he will replace narrative with description, in which the immobility of the phenomena described opposes the movement of the words. This leads to strange descriptive tales such as

"The Island of the Fay," or "The Domain or Arnheim," or "Landor's Cottage," in which Poe introduces a succession of events after the fact; however, this succession belongs to the process of observation, not to the phenomenon observed. Still more importantly, this same tendency transforms "narrative" tales into a discontinuous juxtaposition of immobile moments. What is "The Masque of the Red Death," if not a static arrangement of three tableaux: the ball, the troubling masque, the spectacle of death? Or "William Wilson," in which a whole life is reduced to a few moments described with the greatest precision? Or "Berenice," in which a long narrative in past tenses indicating repeated actions rather than unique ones is followed by the image of the dead woman and then – after a line of suspension points – by a description of the narrator's room? In the pause – in the white space on the page – the essential is played out: the violation of the sepulcher, Berenice's awakening, the mad act that has brought her teeth to an ebony box lying on Egaeus's desk. The only presence is that of the immobility that makes it possible to guess at the whirlwind of actions.

Poe describes fragments of a whole; and, within these fragments, he chooses the detail; thus in rhetorical terms he practices a double synecdoche. Dostoevsky had pointed out this feature too: "There is in his imaginative faculty a peculiarity that exists nowhere else: the power of the details."[14] The human body in particular is reduced to one of its components; thus, for example, Berenice's teeth: "They were here, and there, and everywhere, and visibly and palpably before me; long, narrow and excessively white, with the pale lips writhing about them, as in the very moment of their first terrible development" (646). Or the eye of the old man in "The Tell-Tale Heart": "One of his eyes resembled that of a vulture – a pale blue eye, with a film over it. . . . I saw it with perfect distinctness – all a dull blue, with a hideous veil over it that chilled the very marrow in my bones" (303–5; this old man consists of an eye and a beating heart, nothing more). We cannot forget, either, the missing eye of the black cat.

Receiving such a charge, the detail ceases to be a way of creating the feeling of reality (as it will be for Flaubert or for Tolstoy, for example), and becomes allegory. The allegory lends itself well to the disappearance of narrative that is characteristic of Poe: as a deployment in depth and not on the surface, allegory has affinities with immobility, thus with description. All Poe's work is propelled by a tendency toward allegory (which explains, in passing, why psychoanalytic criticism, the principal modern form of allegorical criticism, is infatuated with Poe). Certain tales are self-declared allegories (one – "King Pest" – has as its subtitle, "A Tale Containing an Allegory"): for example "Silence – A Fable," "The Oval Portrait," "Some Words with a Mummy," or "William Wilson;" others, more subtly, are open to allegorical interpretation without necessarily demanding it (for example "Ligeia" or even "The Purloined Letter").

---

[14] *Récits, chroniques et polémiques,* 1092.

The third (and not least significant) consequence of Poe's essential choice is that his tales tend to take literature as their object: they are metaliterary tales. Such a sustained attention to the logic of narrative impels him to make narrative itself one of his themes. We have already noted the existence of tales built upon embedded images of themselves. More importantly, numerous stories adopt the parodic tone, being directed as much toward an earlier text or genre as toward their apparent object: these are, once again, the grotesque tales, of which Baudelaire translated only a few. Public acquaintance with them has clearly suffered from the fact that they presuppose familiarity with a particular literary tradition.

Poe is thus, in every sense, a writer of limits – which is at once his principal merit and, if one may say so, his own limit. A creator of new forms, an explorer of unknown spaces, yes; but his production is necessarily marginal. Fortunately, in every age there are readers who prefer the margins to the center.

9 *Heart of Darkness*

On the surface, Joseph Conrad's *Heart of Darkness* resembles an adventure story. As a little boy, Marlow daydreams about the blank spaces on a map. When he grows up he decides to explore the largest of these spaces: the heart of the dark continent, reached by a serpentine river. He is assigned the task of reaching Kurtz, an agent of an ivory-collecting company. He is warned of dangers. This conventional beginning does not keep its promises, however. The risks suggested by the Company's doctor are internal: he measures the cranium of those who set out to travel and asks if there is madness in the family. Similarly, the Swedish captain who takes Marlow to the first station is pessimistic about the future, but he has in mind a man who went off alone and hung himself. Danger lies within; adventures are played out in the explorer's mind, not in the situations he encounters.

What follows only confirms this impression. When Marlow finally reaches the Central Station, he is condemned to inactivity by the shipwreck of the steamboat he is supposed to command. Long months go by during which his only activity is waiting for the arrival of some missing rivets. Nothing happens. And when something finally does happen, the narrative neglects to tell us about it. Kurtz's departure for the station, his meeting with the manager of the Central Station, Marlow's return and his relations with the "pilgrims" after Kurtz's death – all these go unnarrated. During the decisive scene in which Kurtz is found, Marlow remains on board the boat in conversation with a peculiar Russian fellow; we never do find out what happened on land.

Or let us take the traditionally climactic moment in adventure stories, the battle scene: here it takes place between blacks and whites. The only death deemed worthy of mention is the helmsman's, and Marlow speaks of it only because the dying man's blood fills his shoes, which he then flings overboard. The outcome of the battle is derisory: the whites' fire reaches no one and only produces smoke ("I had seen, from the way the tops of the bushes rustled and flew, that almost all the shots had gone too high" [52–3]).[1] As for the blacks,

---

[1] Joseph Conrad, *Heart of Darkness: An Authoritative Text; Backgrounds and Sources;*

103

the mere sound of the boat's whistle sends them flying: "The tumult of angry and warlike yells was checked instantly . . . The retreat . . . was caused by the screeching of the steamwhistle" (47, 53).

The same is true of the one other culminating moment in the story: the unforgettable image of the black woman emerging from the jungle while Kurtz is being lifted into the boat: "Suddenly she opened her bared arms and threw them up rigid about her head, as though in an uncontrollable desire to touch the sky . . ." (62). The gesture is powerful but finally just an enigmatic sign, not an act.

If there is adventure in this story, it is not where we expected to find it. The events that ought to have gripped our attention cannot do so for, contrary to all laws of suspense, their outcome is announced well in advance, and repeatedly. At the very beginning of the voyage, Marlow forewarns his listeners: "I foresaw that in the blinding sunshine of that land I would become acquainted with a flabby, pretending, weak-eyed devil of a rapacious and pitiless folly" (17). We are reminded on several occasions not only of Kurtz's death but also of Marlow's subsequent destiny ("as it turned out, it was to have the care of his memory" [51]).

The facts are unimportant; only their interpretation will count. Marlow's voyage had but one goal: "I had travelled all this way for the sole purpose of talking with Mr. Kurtz. Talking with . . ." (48). Talking in order to comprehend, not to act. That is doubtless why Marlow goes looking for Kurtz after Kurtz has fled from the pilgrims, though Marlow disapproves of the pilgrims' kidnapping: it is because Kurtz has escaped from sight, from earshot, has not allowed himself to be known. The trip up the river is thus a way of approaching truth. Space symbolizes time; the story's adventures foster understanding. "Going up that river was like travelling back to the earliest beginnings of the world . . ." (34). "We were travelling in the night of first ages . . ." (36).

The "mythological" narrative (of action) is present only to allow the deployment of a "gnoseological" narrative (of knowledge). *Acts* are insignificant here because all efforts are focused on the search for *being*. (As Conrad noted in a 1918 article on British seamen: "There is nothing more futile under the sun than a mere adventurer."[2]) Conrad's adventurer – if we want to keep on calling him that – has transformed the direction of his search: he no longer seeks to win but to know.

Countless details strewn throughout the story confirm the predominance of knowing over doing, for the overall design has its repercussions on an infinite number of specific acts that all tend in the same direction. The characters never stop meditating on the hidden meaning of the words they hear, the impene-

Essays in Criticism, ed. Robert Kimbrough (New York: W. W. Norton, 1963). All passages cited are from this edition.
[2] Joseph Conrad, "Well Done" *(The Daily Chronicle,* 1918), in *Notes on Life and Letters* (Garden City, NY and Toronto: Doubleday, Page & Company, 1921) 190. Cited in *Heart of Darkness* (Kimbrough ed.) 138.

trable signification of the signals they perceive. The manager ends all his
sentences with a smile that resembles "a seal applied on the words to make
the meaning of the commonest phrase appear absolutely inscrutable" (*Heart
of Darkness,* 22). The message from the Russian, which is supposed to help
the travelers, is for no obvious reason written in a telegraphic style that renders
it incomprehensible. Kurtz knows the language of the blacks, yet to the question: "Do you understand this?" he merely produces "a smile of indefinable
meaning" (68), a smile as enigmatic as the words spoken in an unknown
language.

If words require interpretation, the nonverbal symbols exchanged need
it even more. During the boat trip up the river, "at night sometimes the
roll of drums behind the curtain of trees would run up the river and remain sustained faintly, as if hovering in the air high over our heads, till
the first break of day. Whether it meant war, peace, or prayer we could
not tell" (35–6). Other symbolic nonintentional phenomena – events, behavior, situations – are just as hard to decipher. The steamer sank to the
bottom of the river: "I did not see the real significance of that wreck at
once" (21). The pilgrims strolled about aimlessly at the Central Station: "I
asked myself sometimes what it all meant" (23). Moreover, Marlow's
profession – steering a boat – is nothing but an ability to interpret signs:
"I had to keep guessing at the channel; I had to discern, mostly by inspiration, the signs of hidden banks; I watched for sunken stones . . . I had to
keep a look-out for the signs of dead wood we could cut up in the night for
next day's steaming. When you have to attend to things of that sort, to the
mere incidents of the surface, the reality – the reality, I tell you – fades. The
inner truth is hidden – luckily, luckily"(34). Truth, reality, essences remain
intangible; life wears itself out in the interpretation of signs.

Human relationships can be summed up as hermeneutic research. The Russian, for Marlow, is "inexplicable," "an insoluble problem" (55). Yet Marlow
himself becomes an object of interpretation for the brickmaker. And the Russian in turn, speaking of the relationship between Kurtz and his wife, has to
admit defeat: "I don't understand" (63). The jungle itself appears to Marlow
"so dark, so impenetrable to human thought" (56; note that the reference is
to the mind and not the body) that he thinks he detects in it the presence of
a "mute spell" (67).

Several emblematic episodes add to the evidence that we are dealing with
a narrative in which the interpretation of symbols predominates. At the beginning, at the gates of the Company, in a European city, two women are
found: "Often far away there I thought of these two, guarding the door of
Darkness, knitting black wool as for a warm pall, one introducing, introducing
continuously to the unknown, the other scrutinizing the cheery and foolish
faces with unconcerned old eyes" (11). The one seeks (passively) to know; the
other directs inquirers toward a knowledge that eludes her: these two figures
of knowledge announce the unfolding of the narrative to come. At the very
end of the story, we find another symbolic image: Kurtz's Intended dreams

of what she could have done if she had been with him: "I would have treasured every sigh, every word, every sign, every glance" (78): she would have made a collection of signs.

Marlow's narrative opens, moreover, with a parable featuring not Kurtz and the dark continent but an imaginary Roman, conqueror of England in the Year One. The Roman encounters the same savagery, the same mystery; what he confronts is beyond comprehension. "He has to live in the midst of the incomprehensible, which is also detestable. And it has a fascination, too, that goes to work upon him" (6). The tale that follows, illustrating the general case, is thus a tale of apprenticeship in the art of interpretation.

The ample and obvious metaphorics of black and white, light and dark, is clearly not unrelated to the problem of knowing. In principle, and in keeping with the metaphors inscribed in the English language, darkness is equivalent to ignorance, light to knowledge. England in its obscure beginnings is summed up in the word "darkness." The manager's enigmatic smile produces the same effect. "He sealed the utterance with that smile of his, as though it had been a door opening into a darkness he had in his keeping" (22). Conversely, Kurtz's story illuminates Marlow's existence: "It seemed somehow to throw a kind of light on everything about me – and into my thoughts. It was sombre enough, too – and pitiful – not extraordinary in any way – not very clear either. No, not very clear. And yet it seemed to throw a kind of light" (7).

The title of the story has the same metaphoric resonance. The expression "heart of darkness" recurs several times in the text; it designates the interior of the unknown continent where the steamer is headed ("We penetrated deeper and deeper into the heart of darkness" [35]) or from which it is returning ("The brown current ran swiftly out of the heart of darkness" [69]). It also is used in a restrictive sense to designate the man who embodies the continent's untouchable core – Kurtz as he lives in Marlow's memory while Marlow is crossing the threshold of the Intended's house (75). It appears again in the last sentence of the text, referring by generalization to the place of unconsciousness toward which another river flows: "into the heart of an immense darkness" (79). In its metonymic usage, darkness also symbolizes danger or despair.

The status of darkness is actually more ambiguous than one might think at first, for it becomes an object of desire; light, in turn, is identified with presence, in all its frustrating aspects. Kurtz, the object of desire of the entire narrative, is himself an "impenetrable darkness." He identifies to such an extent with the darkness that, when there is a light beside him, he does not notice it. " 'I am lying here in the dark waiting for death.' The light was within a foot of his eyes" (70). And when a light is on in the night, Kurtz cannot be present: "A light was burning within, but Mr. Kurtz was not there" (65). This ambiguity of light is best revealed in Kurtz's death scene. Watching him die, Marlow blows out the candles: Kurtz belongs to darkness. Yet immediately afterward, Marlow takes refuge in the lighted cabin and refuses to leave, even though the others may accuse him of insensitivity: "There was a lamp in there

– light, don't you know – and outside it was so beastly, beastly dark" (71). Light is reassuring when darkness escapes.

The same ambiguity characterizes the division between black and white. In harmony, once again, with the metaphors of the language, the unknown is described as black. We have already observed the two women at the entrance to the Company knitting with black wool. The unknown continent is black ("the edge of a colossal jungle, so dark-green as to be almost black" [13]), as is the skin of its inhabitants. Significantly, those blacks who enter into contact with whites are contaminated: inevitably, they have some spot of whiteness. This is the case with the paddlers who go in small boats between the continent and the steamer: the boats were "paddled by black fellows. You could see from afar the white of their eyeballs glistening" (13–14). Or those who work for the whites: "It looked startling round his black neck, this bit of white thread from beyond the seas" (18). Danger is black, too, even to the point of comedy: a Danish captain gets killed because of two hens. "Yes, two black hens" (9).

And yet whiteness is not a straightforward object of desire, any more than light is: blackness is desired, and whiteness is only the disappointing result of a desire that proclaims itself satisfied. Whiteness will be disavowed, as a truth that is either deceptive (as with the white spaces on the map, which hide the black continent) or illusory: the whites think that ivory, white, is the ultimate truth; but Marlow exclaims: "I've never seen anything so unreal in my life" (23). Whiteness may be an obstacle to knowledge, as with the white fog, "more blinding than the night" (40), which impedes the approach to Kurtz. White, finally, is the white man confronting the black: and all Conrad's paternalistic ethnocentrism (which could pass for anticolonialism in the nineteenth century) cannot keep us from seeing that his sympathy lies with the indigenous inhabitants of the black continent: whites are cruel and stupid. Kurtz, ambiguous with respect to light and darkness, is equally so with respect to white and black. For on the one hand, believing that he possesses the truth, he advocates white domination of the blacks, in his report; and even the head of this tireless ivory hunter has become "like a ball – an ivory ball" (49). On the other hand, he flees from whites, and wants to stay with the blacks; it is not a coincidence that Marlow, speaking of his meeting with Kurtz, alludes to "the peculiar blackness of that experience" (66).

The narrative is thus impregnated with black and white, obscurity and clarity, for these shades are coordinated with the process of acquiring knowledge – and with its converse, ignorance, with all the nuances that these two terms can include. It all comes down to knowing, even colors and shadows. But nothing reveals the power of knowing better than Kurtz's role in the story. For the text is in fact the account of the search for Kurtz: the reader learns this little by little, and retrospectively. Knowledge of Kurtz provides the gradation on which the story is constructed. Just after the transition from the first chapter to the second, Marlow says: "As for me, I seemed to see Kurtz for the first time" (32); and the transition from the second chapter to the third is marked by Marlow's encounter with the Russian, of all the characters in the book the one who knew Kurtz best. Moreover, Kurtz is far from being the only subject of the first chapter, whereas he dominates the second; in the third, finally, we encounter episodes that have nothing to do with the river voyage but that contribute to our knowledge of Kurtz, for example Marlow's subsequent encounters with Kurtz's next of kin, and the inquiries of all those who are trying to find out who he was. Kurtz is the pole of attraction of the narrative as a whole; however, it is only after the fact that we discover just how this attraction works. Kurtz is darkness, the object of desire of the narration; the heart of darkness is "the barren darkness of his heart" (69). As we might have guessed, when he takes up painting, he paints darkness and light: "a small sketch in oils, on a panel, representing a woman, draped and blindfolded, carrying a lighted torch. The background was sombre – almost black" (25).

Kurtz is indeed the focal point of the narrative, and knowledge of Kurtz is the driving force of the plot. Yet Kurtz's status within the story is quite peculiar. We have virtually no direct perception of him at all. Throughout most of the text his presence is anticipated, like that of a creature one is striving to reach but cannot yet see. After Marlow first hears about him, several sequential narratives describe him – the accountant's, the manager's, the bricklayer's. These narratives, whether they are grounded in admiration or terror, all make us want to know Kurtz, but they do not tell us much beyond the fact that there is something to be told. Then comes the trip upriver, supposed to lead us to the real Kurtz. Obstacles proliferate, however: darkness first of all, the attack by the blacks, the thick fog that prevents the travelers from seeing anything. At this point in the text, specifically narrative obstacles compound those thrown up by the jungle: instead of pursuing his tale of progressive knowledge of Kurtz, Marlow interrupts himself abruptly and sketches in a retrospective portrait, as if Kurtz can only be present in the tenses of absence, past and future. This is made explicit, moreover, after Marlow, who has just seen Kurtz, declares: " 'I think Mr. Kurtz is a remarkable man,' " the manager responds: " 'he *was*' " (63). When we return from portrait to narrative, new disappointments await us: in place of Kurtz we find the Russian, the author of a new story about the absent hero. Even when Kurtz finally appears, we do not learn very much. In the first place, he is dying, already partaking more of absence than of presence. Furthermore, we see him from afar, and fleetingly. When we are finally allowed into his presence, he is reduced to mere voice – thus to words, which are just as subject to interpretation as were the stories others had told about him. Yet another wall has arisen between Kurtz and ourselves. "Kurtz discoursed. A voice! a voice! It rang deep to the last" (69). It is hardly surprising that this voice is particularly impressive: "The volume of tone he emitted without effort, almost without the trouble of moving his lips, amazed me. A voice! a voice! It was grave, profound. vibrating, while the man did not seem capable of a whisper" (61). But even this enigmatic presence does not last, and soon a "veil" descends over his face, rendering it impenetrable. Death changes almost nothing, so impossible had knowledge proved during Kurtz's life. We have merely moved from speculating to remembering.

Thus not only does the process of coming to know Kurtz dominate Marlow's narrative, but the knowledge sought is unattainable. Kurtz has become familiar to us, but we do not know him, we do not know his secret. Conrad expresses this frustration in dozens of different ways. In the end, Marlow has only been able to pursue a shadow, "the shade of Mr. Kurtz" (50): "a shadow darker than the shadow of the night, and draped nobly in the folds of a gorgeous eloquence" (75). The heart of darkness is "Nowhere," and it cannot be reached. Kurtz fades away before it is possible to know him ("all that had been Kurtz's had passed out of my hands: his soul, his body, his station, his plans, his ivory, his career. There remained only his memory . . ." [74]). His name, Kurtz, "short," is only superficially misleading. When Marlow sees him for the first time, he remarks: "Kurtz – Kurtz – that means short in German – don't it? Well, the name was as true as everything else in his life – and death. He looked at least seven feet long" (60). Kurtz is not small, as his name might suggest; it is our knowledge of him that falls short, remains forever inadequate, and it is no accident that he resists the whites' efforts to drag him out of his obscurity. Marlow has not understood Kurtz, even though he becomes his confidant at the end ("this . . . wraith . . . honoured me with its amazing confidence" [50]); similarly, after Kurtz's death, Marlow's efforts to understand him come to nothing: "even the cousin . . . could not tell me what he had been – exactly" (73).

Kurtz is the heart of darkness and his heart is empty. One can only dream about the ultimate moment, at the threshold of death, when one acquires absolute knowledge ("that supreme moment of complete knowledge" [71]). What Kurtz actually utters at that moment are words that express the void, canceling out knowledge: "The horror! The horror!" (ibid.). An absolute horror whose object we shall never know.

Nothing is better proof of the derisory nature of knowledge than the final scene of the story, Marlow's meeting with the Intended. It is she who says " 'I knew him best' " (76); yet we know that her knowledge is hopelessly incomplete, even illusory. Nothing remains of Kurtz but his memory, and this memory is false. When the Intended exclaims: " 'How true! How true!' " (ibid.), it is in response to a lie. " 'His words, at least, have not died' " (78), she says to console herself; and a moment later she extracts from Marlow another lie, about Kurtz's last words: " 'The last word he pronounced was – your name' . . . 'I knew it – I was sure!' " (79), the Intended replies. Is that why, in the course of the conversation, "with every word spoken, the room was growing darker" (76)?

Knowledge is impossible; the heart of darkness is itself obscure: this is the burden of the text as a whole. The voyage takes us indeed to the very center, the interior, the bottom, the core: "I felt as though, instead of going to the centre of a continent, I were about to set off for the centre of the earth" (13); Kurtz's station is appropriately called the Inner Station; Kurtz himself is indeed "at the very bottom of there" (19). But the center is empty: "An empty stream, a great silence, an impenetrable forest" (34). According to the manager, " 'Men who come out here should have no entrails' " (22); this rule proves to be followed to the letter. Marlow says of the brickmaker: "It seemed to me that if I tried I could poke my forefinger through him, and would find nothing inside . . ." (26). The manager himself, as we recall, stamps everything with an enigmatic smile; but perhaps his secret is impenetrable because it does not exist: "He never gave that secret away. Perhaps there was nothing within him" (22).

The interior does not exist, any more than does ultimate meaning, and Marlow's experiences are all inconclusive. In this context, the very act of knowing is called into question. "Droll thing life is – that mysterious arrangement of merciless logic for a futile purpose. The most you can hope from it is some knowledge of yourself – that comes too late – a crop of unextinguishable regrets" (71). The machine functions perfectly – but it is empty, and the fullest knowledge of others tells us only about ourselves. That the process of acquiring knowledge unfolds in an irreproachable manner in no way proves that the object of this knowledge may be reached; one is tempted to say indeed that just the opposite is true. E. M. Forster failed to understand this, for he remarked about Conrad, in perplexity: "What is so elusive about him is that he is always promising to make some general philosophical statement about the universe, and then refraining in a gruff declaimer . . . There is a central obscurity about him, something noble, heroic, inspiring half-a-dozen great books, but obscure! Obscure!"[3] We already know what to make of this obscurity. And Conrad himself wrote elsewhere: "The aim of art . . . is not in the clear logic of a triumphant conclusion; it is not in the unveiling of one of those heartless secrets which are called the Laws of Nature."[4]

Speech, as we have seen, plays a decisive role in the process of acquiring knowledge: that is the light that ought to dispel darkness but in the end fails to do so. This we learn from Kurtz's example. "Of all his gifts the one that stood out preeminently, that carried with it a sense of real presence, was his ability to talk, his words – the gift of expression, the bewildering, the illuminating, the most exalted and the most contemptible, the pulsating stream of light, or the deceitful flow from the heart of an impenetrable darkness" (*Heart of Darkness,* 48). But Kurtz only exemplifies something much more general, which is the possibility of constructing a reality, of stating a truth by means of words; Kurtz's adventure is at the same time a parable of narrative. It is no coincidence that Kurtz is also, as the occasion warrants, a poet, painter, and musician as well. It is not an accident that countless analogies are set up

[3] E.M. Forster, cited in *Heart of Darkness* (Kimbrough ed.) 164.
[4] Joseph Conrad, Preface, *The Nigger of the "Narcissus,"* in *The Works of Joseph Conrad,* vol. 3 (London: William Heinemann, 1921) xi–xii.

between the two narratives, the embedded tale and the framing tale, between the two rivers, finally between Kurtz and Marlow the narrator (the only two characters that have proper names in this story; all the others, such as the manager and the accountant – whom we meet moreover both in the framing story and in the embedded one – are reduced to their functions), and, correlatively, between Marlow the character and his listeners (whose role is played by ourselves, the readers). Kurtz is a voice. "I made the strange discovery that I had never imagined him as doing, you know, but as discoursing. I didn't say to myself, 'Now I will never see him,' or 'Now I will never shake him by the hand,' but 'now I will never hear him.' The man presented himself as a voice" (ibid.). But is not the same thing true of Marlow the narrator? "For a long time already he, sitting apart, had been no more to us than a voice" (28). "The artist . . . is so much of a voice that, for him, silence is like death," Conrad wrote in a 1905 article on Henry James.[5] Marlow does the job of making the relation between the two series explicit in an interruption in his narrative: "Kurtz . . . was just a word for me. I did not see the man in the name any more than you do. Do you see him? Do you see the story? Do you see anything?" (27). Both explorer and reader are concerned only with signs, on the basis of which they have to construct, respectively, the referent (the reality that lies all around) or the reference (what the story is about). The reader (any reader) desires to know the object of the story just as Marlow desires to know Kurtz.

And just as this latter desire will be frustrated, so readers or listeners will never be able to reach the reference of the narrative, as we would have liked; its heart is quite absent. Is it not revealing that the story, begun at sunset, coincides in its development with the deepening dusk? "It had become so pitch dark that we listeners could hardly see one another" (28). And just as knowledge of Kurtz is impossible in Marlow's account, so too is any construction on the basis of words, any attempt to grasp things through language. "No, it is impossible; it is impossible to convey the life-sensation of any given epoch of one's existence – that which makes its truth, its meaning – its subtle and penetrating essence. It is impossible" (ibid.). The essence, the truth – the heart of the story – is inaccessible, the reader will never reach it. "You can't understand" (50). Words do not allow us even to transmit other words: "I've been telling you what we said – repeating the phrases we pronounced – but what's the good? They were common everyday words – the familiar, vague sounds exchanged on every waking day of life. But what of that? They had behind them, to my mind, the terrific suggestiveness of words heard in dreams, of phrases spoken in nightmares" (67). This aspect of words can never be reproduced.

It is impossible to accede to the reference; the heart of the story is empty, just as is the heart of man. For Marlow, "the meaning of an episode was not

---

[5] Joseph Conrad, "Henry James: An Appreciation" (*North American Review,* 1905), in *Notes on Life and Letters,* 14. Cited in *Heart of Darkness* (Kimbrough ed.) 148.

inside like a kernel but outside, enveloping the tale which brought it out only as a glow brings out a haze, in the likeness of one of these misty halos that sometimes are made visible by the spectral illumination of moonshine" (5). The story's light is the hesitant light of the moon.

Thus Kurtz's story symbolizes the fact of fiction, construction on the basis of an absent center. Let us make no mistake: Conrad's writing is indeed allegorical, as numerous details attest (if only the absence of proper names, a way of generalizing), but not all allegorical interpretations of *Heart of Darkness* are equally welcome. To reduce the trip up the river to a descent into hell or to the discovery of the unconscious is an assertion for which the critic who utters it must take full responsibility. Conrad's allegorism is intertextual: if the search for Kurtz's identity is an allegory of reading, this allegory in turn symbolizes every quest for knowledge – knowledge of Kurtz being one example. The symbolized becomes in turn the symbolizer for what was formerly symbolizing; the symbolization is reciprocal. A final meaning, ultimate truth, is nowhere to be found, for there is no interior and the heart is empty. What was true for things remains so, and more so, for signs; there is only referral, circular and nonetheless imperative, from one surface to another, from words to words.

10 *The Awkward Age*

What is *The Awkward Age* about? This apparently elementary question is not easy to answer. As readers, we cannot be quite sure; our only consolation is that the characters themselves seem to have just as much trouble understanding what people tell them as we do.

A large proportion of the dialogue in this novel – which is made up almost exclusively of talk – in fact consists of requests for explanation. These requests may be questions about various aspects of discourse; they may bring to light a number of different reasons for obscurity. The first, the simplest and least common, lies in uncertainty about the very meanings of words. This is what a foreigner who knows the language imperfectly would normally experience; here the questions focus on vocabulary. Although no foreigner with limited English appears in *The Awkward Age,* one character, Mr. Longdon, has spent a long time living far from the city. Upon returning he has the impression that he no longer understands what words mean, and at least during his early conversations he asks questions like: " 'What do you mean by early?' " or " 'What do you mean by the strain?' "[1] Such questions, innocent enough in appearance, nevertheless oblige those to whom they are addressed both to clarify their meanings and to take full responsibility for them; this is why the questions sometimes provoke vigorous refusals. " 'What do you mean by fast?' " asks the same Mr. Longdon, but the duchess gives a curt reply: " 'Why should I mean but what I say?' " (214). However, as we shall see, the Duchess's own niece is afflicted with the same disability; she cannot understand the meaning of words.

In a second verbal scenario, much more frequent and in itself quite complex, the explanations requested do not concern the meaning of words but their application to a concrete situation: the meaning is known but not the referent. In the most elementary cases, the hearer's ignorance is due to the overly elliptical character of the initial utterance, which lacks some complement that would have allowed the hearer to determine its realm of application. Here are examples of such exchanges: " 'Ah, but with your ideas that doesn't prevent.'

---

[1] Henry James, *The Awkward Age* (New York and London: Harper and Brothers, 1899) 22.

'Prevent what?' 'Why, what you call, I suppose, *pourparlers.*' 'For Aggie's hand?' " (49). " 'It's sweet her sparing one!' 'Do you mean about talking before her?' " (137). " 'Shall *I* inquire?' But Vanderbank, with another thought, had lost the thread. 'Inquire what?' 'Why, if she does get anything – ' 'If I'm not kind *enough?* ' – Van had caught up" (315).

Sometimes the utterance is not exactly elliptical but is rather larded with anaphoric and deictic pronouns whose antecedent or referent is unknown; the question "What do you mean?" obviously does not concern a pronoun's meaning but its reference. " 'He has taken the greatest fancy to him.' 'The old man, to Van?' 'Van, to Mr. Longdon' " (63). " 'What *is* there between her and him?' Mitchy wondered at the other two. 'Between Edward and the girl?' 'Don't talk nonsense. Between Petherton and Jane' " (70). " 'But what is she up to?' It was apparently for Mrs. Brook a question of such a variety of application that she brought out experimentally: 'Jane?' 'Dear, no' " (371). The distance between what the various interlocutors have in mind may be considerable: " 'Would you mind finding out?' . . . Do you mean who's to dine?' 'No, that doesn't matter. But whether Mitchy *has* come down' " (60). Mitchy, highly skilled himself in the art of ellipsis, begins a conversation this way: " 'Well, has he done it?' " (387).

Anaphoric pronouns are only the most eloquent example of this referential vagueness that also affects other sorts of expressions. The metalinguistic question they raise no longer consists in speculating about proper names as possible antecedents, but in asking, more vaguely: " 'What do you call . . . ' " (11). " 'I give you up to your fate.' 'What do you call my fate?' 'Oh, something dreadful – ' " (35). " 'I want you to do with me exactly as you do with him.' 'Ah, that's soon said,' the girl replied in a peculiar tone. 'How do you mean, to 'do'?' " (173). The duchess again refuses to enlighten Mr. Longdon: " 'She favors Mr. Mitchett because she wants 'old Van' herself.' 'In what sense – herself?' 'Ah, you must supply the sense, I can give you only the fact' " (210). Naturally, these different forms of vagueness are quite often compounded within a single sentence: " 'Do you mean you *really* don't know if she gets it?' 'The money, if he doesn't go in?' " (262). " 'He must take the consequence.' 'He?' . . . 'I mean Mr. Longdon.' 'And what do you mean by the consequence?' " (275). And there is no guarantee that the referent can always be discovered. What is Nanda talking about when she says to Vanderbank: " 'It's the tone and the current and the effect of all the others that push you along [but where?]. If such things [what things?] are contagious, as everyone says, you prove it [what?] perhaps as much as anyone' " (288). Or, to Mitchy: " 'It's quite what I believe, only there's ever so much more. More *has* come – and more will yet. You see, when there has been nothing before, it all has to come with a rush' " (444). We wait in vain for a hint of some kind that will allow us to anchor these airy phrases to the earth.

There is also a symmetrically opposite situation in which, instead of starting with an expression and trying to determine its referent, the speaker starts with some thing and tries to find out what it is called. " 'I thought it had a sort of something-or-other.' 'A sort of a morbid modernity?' . . . 'Is that what they call it? Awfully good name' " (66). Or else two names for the same object are contrasted: " 'Do you call Tishy Grendon a woman?' . . . 'What do *you* call her?' . . . 'Why, Nanda's best friend' " (45). Sometimes the abrupt juxtaposition of the thing's ordinary name and its precise designation (a trope) produces a humorous effect. " 'We can't be Greeks if we would.' 'Do you call Granny a Greek?' " (178). " 'When you're satisfied a woman's 'really' poor, do you never give her a crust?' 'Do you call Nanda a crust, Duchess?' " (345–6). One of Nanda's characteristic features or – it amounts to the same thing – one of the distinctive features of her conversation is a certain indifference to the words she uses, as long as the things referred to remain the same. " 'Oh, I don't know that it matters much what it's called,' " she says to her mother (274), and to Mr. Longdon: " 'I'm glad I'm anything – whatever you may call it, and though I can't call it the same – that's good for *you*' " (453).

In the first case, then, the speaker inquires about the meaning of words and remains at the level of language; in the second instance, moving to the perspective of discourse, the speaker questions the relation between words and what they designate. But the third case is at once the most frequently encountered and the most interesting. Here the meaning of words is understood; the referent is known; but there is uncertainty as to whether the words mean what they seem to mean or are being used instead to refer indirectly to something quite different. Society as represented in *The Awkward Age* cultivates indirect expression, and Mrs. Brook calls one of her friends her " 'comrade in obliquity' " (375). Nanda, aware of the capacity of words to take on new properties, invites this attitude toward her own discourse: " 'One must let the sense of all that I speak of – well, all come' " (450).

Indirect or symbolic use of discourse characterizes a great variety of cases, but we can begin by separating two sorts, lexical symbolism and propositional symbolism, according to whether the initial assertion is abolished or maintained. The first instance is that of tropes, and it is astonishing to find so few examples (is this characteristic of all conversation, or only of Mrs. Brook's circle?), all the more so because tropes are always accompanied by a translation. It is Mr. Longdon again who persists in not understanding tropes. For example, Mitchy tells him: " 'Let me have a finger in it,' " and, seeing the other's perplexity, explains: " 'I mean – let me help' " (107). Or, in another conversation: " 'Mrs. Grendon's broken nose, sir,' Vanderbank explained to Mr. Longdon, 'is only the kinder way taken by these ladies to speak of Mrs. Grendon's broken heart.' " Here Vanderbank translates the invented metaphor by a commonplace metonymy; however, Mr. Longdon himself supplies the literal expression in his response: " 'Mr. Grendon does not like her' " (345). When the trope is not followed by its translation, the narrator takes pains at least to point it out with a rhetorical term: "the Duchess's image" (87); "she spoke without attention to this hyperbole" (116); "Mrs. Brook, on a quick survey, selected the ironic" (143).

The only trope used regularly in these worldly conversations is euphemism.

More precisely, in order to avoid hurting someone's feelings but also to show one's own reserve or discretion, one slips from the name of the thing, a name that conveys a judgment, to a generic term which has neither positive or negative value. Here is an example of the positive sort: " 'He has said a great deal to me of your mother.' 'Oh, everything that's kind, of course – or you wouldn't have mentioned it.' 'That's what I mean' " (284–5). The negative version is particularly well illustrated by the meaning the word *different* and its equivalents takes on in this social context: to say that someone is different suggests that he is far from perfect. " 'Nothing could be less like her than your manner and your talk,' " Mr. Longdon says to Nanda, who interprets: " 'They're not so good, you must think' " (126). " 'I can't be *you,* certainly, Van.' . . . 'I know what you mean by that. . . . You mean I'm hypocrital' " (151). If the word *different* is to be used without a pejorative nuance, the speaker must so specify: " 'The way to flatter him,' Mitchy declared, 'is . . . to let him see how different you perceive he can bear to think you. I mean of course without hating you' " (304).

But it is propositional rather than lexical symbolism that dominates these conversations. An initial utterance need not be rejected, but it may turn out to be only the starting point for associations leading to a new utterance. In the novel, this way of speaking is identified by such terms as *allusion, insinuation, suggestion.* Here is an example. Mitchy has asked the duchess to explain one of her opinions about Nanda. Instead of answering, the duchess questions him in turn: " 'Pray, on what ground of right, in such a connection, do you do anything of the sort?' " (84). Mitchy, who has understood perfectly well the meaning of the words in the sentence, who has been able to identify their referents, thinks he sees a third dimension, which is precisely an implication, and which he makes explicit by asking yet another question: " 'Do you mean that when a girl liked by a fellow likes him so little in return – ?' " (84). This request for explanation is itself elliptical, but we have no difficulty completing the sentence: "that person does not have the right to ask that sort of question?" Retrospectively, thanks to Mitchy's interpretation, we discover that the duchess's utterance bore a second, implied meaning. Let us analyze the phases we must go through to establish this additional meaning. The duchess's formula is a rhetorical question that could be made explicit if it were converted to a negative statement: "You have no right to act that way, no right to ask me that sort of question." Without Mitchy's help, can we perceive that this sentence is charged with a hidden meaning, and make it explicit? I doubt it. But Mitchy understands that the literal meaning of the duchess's utterance is not sufficiently relevant to justify its existence; this infringement of the rules of communication leads him to look for a second meaning. Thus the act of interpretation is what gives rise to the text's symbolism; the answer brings forth the question. The next step is to identify the implied meaning whose existence has been recognized. To do this, Mitchy falls back on a commonplace, characteristic of the society in question (and also of that of today's reader), that takes the form of an implication. It goes something like this: if you defend a girl's interests in public, you must be on intimate terms. This commonplace need not be actively present in the speakers' minds; it remains entirely implicit until its presence is required for the interpretation of an utterance that would otherwise appear unjustified. Thus one need only utter the first clause of the implication (making it specific through the use of a personal pronoun or a proper noun) in order to call forth the second clause in the listener's mind, in the form of an implied meaning.

For allusion to exist, therefore, three conditions must be met at once. Something must impel us to look for it; an implication must be present in the minds of the two interlocutors; finally, an utterance must introduce it. But these conditions may be satisfied in quite varied ways. To begin with the first, the key to the allusion obviously need not appear in the utterance itself (although it may do so). Every society or microsociety, like Mrs. Brook's drawing room, seems to possess what might be called a threshold of minimal relevance, beneath which all utterances are reinterpreted as allusions (otherwise they would not have been formulated). Failure to observe the rule of relevance is sometimes obvious; for instance, when Mitchy asks Mrs. Brook: " 'And where's the child this time?' " Mrs. Brook is right to question him in turn: " 'Why do you say 'this time'? – as if it were different from any other time!' " (65). But Mrs. Brook's salon has raised the threshold of relevance much higher than ordinary usage demands; for example, when Mrs. Brook says of the duchess: " 'Why, she has never had to pay for *anything!*' " Nanda interprets: " 'You mean that *you* have had to pay – ?' " (265–6). Apparently one cannot say *"X is a,"* unless one means to suggest "but *I* am not"; the implication common to the members of this circle is that one does not assert something about someone unless the contrary is true of oneself. It suffices for a word to be accentuated, emphasized in the response, for it to become obvious that its implications have been grasped. This habit of picking up on terms used by others is very widespread in the salon. For example, Mrs. Brook says to Mitchy: " '*I*'m vulgar, Mitchy dear – very often: and the marvel of you is that you never are.' 'Thank you for everything. Thank you above all for 'marvel',' Mitchy grinned. 'Oh, I know what I say!' – she didn't in the least blush" (72). " 'You've certainly – with your talk about 'warning' – the happiest expressions' " (245). " 'Loyalty' again is exquisite' " (246). " 'Accessible' is good' " (372). Even more generally, in this universe no word is taken for granted. This discourse is *willkürlich,* arbitrary and thus deliberate. All names, all expressions are always possible (or as Vanderbank says: " 'We all call everything – anything' " [227]), and thus always suggestive: things do not justify words, so one must (or at least one may) look for their justification elsewhere, and in particular in *another* meaning.

The interlocutors' common ground may vary too; the important thing is that there be one. It is to this fact, banal in itself but somewhat paradoxical in its expression, that sentences of the following sort refer: " 'Her coming here . . . when she knows I know *she* knows' " (56). " 'I know you know what I've known' " (402). This plethora of knowledge is set in counterpoint to the ignorance in which all the characters are mired regarding the interpretation of individual words. The common ground need not be shared by the social group as a whole, need not even be present in the group's collective memory; it is enough for it to be uttered at the same time by one of two speakers for it to become instantly the property of both. And between the true commonplace (as codified for example in a proverb) and shared knowledge drawn from the immediate context, all the intermediate cases are possible. Mr. Longdon says to Vanderbank: your mother consoled me "more than the others" (25). This utterance is not obviously inscribed within any paradigm of implication common to their social group. But Mr. Longdon's previous remarks provide the key: if a woman consoled me, he says in effect, it was because she did not love me. Vanderbank thus interprets without difficulty: " 'You mean there was a question – ?' " (25). Nanda says to Vanderbank: " 'He liked you from the first.' " Vanderbank interprets: " 'You mean I managed him so well?' " (177). Nanda's remark, like Mr. Longdon's earlier one, does not seem to refer to any common implication, and nothing in the immediate context authorizes Vanderbank to propose his audacious interpretation. Here, the formulation of the implied meaning (certainly imaginary) serves as point of departure for the search for an implication that would justify the interpretation. The first speaker says: *p;* the second replies: therefore *q*?, which leads the first in turn to discover that the assertion "if *p,* then *q*" has been imputed to him. The real hidden meaning here is the underlying implication, for this latter in turn is the point of departure for another implication, which characterizes (incorrectly) Nanda's attitude.

These implications of the utterance (or underlying meanings, or allusions, or suggestions), whether intended by the speaker or imposed by his partner but always produced within a particular discursive context, occupy a middle ground between two phenomena of which one is fairly narrow and the other virtually limitless. The first is represented by a statement's implications or presuppositions: they belong to the language and can be spelled out in advance without recourse to any context at all. For instance, when Mr. Longdon says: " 'Fortunately, the ladies haven't yet come,' " Mitchy can reply without manifesting any complicity or particular refinement: " 'Oh, there *are* to be ladies?' "(99). The undeniability that is characteristic of presuppositions makes them an effective tool for argument; one may even attempt to camouflage what is merely an implication of the utterance as an implication of the sentence itself. Mrs. Brook says: " 'You deny that you've declined, which means then that you've allowed our friend to hope' " (246). Mrs. Brook is confusing contraries and contradictories here, doubtless on purpose; the sentence she is interpreting says that its subject has not refused; but to "accept" or "allow to hope" are only two possible instances of nonrefusal. Mrs. Brook's interpretation is not carried out in the name of linguistic logic, but rather in keeping with a social implication: "if one does not refuse, it means one is ready to accept."

On the other hand we find implications that belong not to the utterance itself but to the enunciatory act, that is, to the event that transpires when certain words are said. Carried away by the conversation he is having with Mr. Longdon, Vanderbank refers to Mrs. Brook as "Fernanda," whereas he never calls her by her first name to her face (10). Mr. Longdon interprets this incident as the clue, let us say, to a certain vulgarity on Vanderbank's part. Such vulgarity is obviously not implied by the mere utterance "Fernanda," but only by the fact that this name has been pronounced in particular circumstances. Here is another example: during the same conversation, Vanderbank says that for some time Mrs. Brook has been making her daughter out to be younger than she is. This remark has an implication that Mr. Longdon understands perfectly well: Mrs. Brook is seeking to make *herself* appear younger (16). But what he retains is something else again, something implied by Vanderbank's act of enunciation: speaking that way *shows* (which is not to say *means*) a lack of loyalty toward one's friends.

The implications of enunciatory acts are hard to delimit, for the verbal nature of the events is contingent: verbal events or enunciations signify in just the same way as all other events, situations or phenomena. For example, when Nanda arrives at Vanderbank's house to find only Mitchy and Mr. Longdon present, she interprets the situation as follows (even though nothing at all has been said): " 'Do you mean to say Van isn't here?' " (108). Mr. Longdon in particular counts on his friends' perspicacity: if they can interpret situations before any words have been spoken, they spare him the disagreeable task of doing it himself. Mitchy manages this quite quickly, whereas Vanderbank, on another occasion, is slower. His interlocutor insists: "Mr. Longdon took up another ash-tray, but with the air of doing so as a direct consequence of Vanderbank's tone. After he had laid it down, he put on his glasses, then, fixing his companion, he brought out: 'Have you no idea at all – ?...Of what you have in your head? Dear Mr. Longdon, how should I?' 'Well, I'm wondering if I shouldn't perhaps have a little in your place. There's nothing that, in the circumstance, occurs to you as likely for me to want to say?' " (217). The intonation, tone, and gestures accompanying speech ensure the continuity between the verbal and nonverbal domains; they are like a nonverbal orchestration of the words. "Nanda replied in a tone evidently marking how much he pleased her" (126). "It was wonderful how her accent discriminated" (140).

To summarize, then, we may say that in order to understand better, the interlocutor asks questions in return: What does that mean? What do you mean by that? What are you talking about? In search of additional clarification, he may even question the enunciatory act itself, may ask someone to spell out what led to the formulation of the utterance; this is also an excellent way to avoid answering questions (we hardly need stress the ambivalence of this gesture, which is intended to block communication as well as to further it). We have already observed an exchange between Mitchy and the duchess illustrating this possibility; here is another example. When the duchess asks: " 'Can I take her any message from you?' " Mitchy responds by questioning the motives behind her question: " 'Why should you dream of her expecting one?' " (93). The refusal to reply is even more overt in the following exchange:

" 'Why . . . did you secure Nanda's return?' . . . 'Fancy your asking me – at this time of day!' " (370).

The conversation may also be deflected by comments on the language used, in an effort to establish its precise value – with the possibility of going on to draw conclusions about the speaker. Thus Vanderbank repeatedly comments on Mrs. Brook's statements: " 'I do so like your phrases!' " (242). " 'How I like your expressions!' " (370). This sort of commentary becomes a way of showing that each character has a particular way of speaking and understanding, a manner that is perceived and discussed in turn by the others. The duchess says of Mitchy: " 'He takes his ease in talk – but that . . . is much a matter of whom he talks with' " (53), whereas Mrs. Brook characterizes him as follows: " 'Your talk's half the time impossible; . . . There's no one with whom, in talking, . . . I find myself half so often suddenly moved to pull up short' " (71). Speaking of Tishy, the duchess is even more severe: " '[Her] conversation has absolutely no limits, [she] says everything that comes into her head' " (46). On the other hand, with Vanderbank, "the art of conversation [had developed] to the point at which he could . . . sustain a lady in the upper air" (159). Mrs. Brook, for her part, would prefer never to *name* things; having to do so causes her infinite regret: " 'I do say the most hideous things. But we *have* said worse, haven't we?' . . . 'Are you thinking of money?' 'Yes. Isn't it awful?' 'That you should think of it?' 'That I should talk this way' " (239).

Even if an individual's discursive tendencies are not mentioned by other characters, the narrator continually brings them to light and occasionally points them out; they are all measured on a scale of interpretive ability. Several of Mr. Longdon's traits have already been noted: he does not allow himself to say anything about an absent person that he would not want repeated in that person's presence; he has what the narrator calls a "habit of not depreciating in private those to whom he was publicly civil" (335) – his way of using proper names is one instance of this. The other characteristic we have already seen is his refusal to grasp hidden meanings or tropes, for any interpretation of this sort would imply knowledge common to the interlocutors, and thus complicity between them. By not understanding, Mr. Longdon refuses precisely this complicity. One of his conversations with the duchess, for example, is punctuated with remarks like this: " 'I'm afraid I don't understand you' " (196); "His apprehension was perhaps imperfect, but it could still lead somehow to his flushing all over" (207); "He stood with his face full of perceptions strained and scattered" (214), for the duchess has scolded him for his refusal of complicity: " 'Don't try to create unnecessary obscurity by being unnecessarily modest' " (210).

Many other characters, like Mr. Longdon, fall outside the norm of perfect comprehension, a norm represented in this novel by Mrs. Brook's circle. What the outsiders all have in common is a lack of full understanding, but this is not necessarily because they refuse to share certain postulates. Four characters in particular suffer from symbolic deafness: Tishy Grendon, little Aggie, Mr. Cashmore, and Edward. The most serious case is that of little Aggie: wonderfully protected by her aunt, the duchess, from all contacts that might corrupt her, she had difficulty not at the level of allusion or reference but at the level of simple meanings of words. Evidence of this is provided in a conversation with Mr. Longdon, even though his language is fairly straightforward. Aggie says: " 'Oh, Nanda, she's my best friend after three or four others.' " Mr. Longdon comments: " 'Don't you think that's rather a back seat, as they say, for one's best friend?' 'A back seat?' she wondered with a purity! 'If you don't understand,' said her companion, 'it serves me right, as your aunt didn't leave me with you to teach you the slang of the day.' 'The 'slang'?' she again spotlessly speculated. 'You've never even heard the expression? I should think that a great compliment to our time if it weren't that I fear it may have been only the name that has been kept from you.' The light of ignorance in the child's smile was positively golden. 'The name?' she again echoed. She understood too little – he gave it up" (199).

Tishy Grendon understands only one thing at a time, while the discourse of her interlocutors goes off in several directions at once; thus she is often several lines behind. Her friend Nanda is her only recourse: " 'Does he mean anything very nasty? I can only understand you when Nanda explains,' she returned to Harold. 'In fact there's scarcely anything I understand except when Nanda explains' " (328). Mr. Cashmore is at once too literal, too explicit in his expression, and too slow to understand, especially when he is talking to Mrs. Brook. "Mr. Cashmore too heavily followed" (138). "Mr. Cashmore wondered – it was almost mystic. 'I don't understand you' " (140). " 'Mercy on us, what *are* you talking about? That's what *I* want to know,' Mr. Cashmore declared vivaciously" (357).

The most subtle variation on symbolic deafness is represented by Edward Brookenham. He understands little better than Mr. Cashmore the web of allusions spun around him by his wife. She addresses a remark to him: "Then as his face told how these *were* involutions, 'You needn't understand, but you can believe me,' she added. . . . It was a statement by which his failure to apprehend was not diminished . . . Edward's gloom, on this, was not quite blankness, yet it was dense" (382). However, his role as master of the house that is the heart of the circle leads him to adopt an attitude that will not betray his lack of understanding. This attitude is obviously silence – which is not however without its own ambiguities. "It was one of [his ways], for instance, that if he was often most silent when most primed with matter, so when he had nothing to say he was always silent too – a misleading peculiarity . . ." (377). Which explains how, in another exchange, nothing gives away his lack of understanding – nor, for that matter, his eventual comprehension." 'Oh!' he simply said. . . . 'Oh!' he merely repeated" (55). " 'Oh!' Brookenham observed" (57). " 'Oh!' replied her husband. . . . 'Oh!' her companion repeated. . . . 'Oh!' her husband again ejaculated" (61–2), and so on.

Alongside these conversational invalids we have Mrs. Brook's circle, where not only is everything understood, but everything may also be said. Indeed, the two basic and complementary rules that govern the use of speech in this drawing room are that one may say anything, and that one must not say anything directly. The duchess calls this, somewhat deprecatingly, " 'your amazing English periodical public washings of dirty linen' " (86), and Nanda, an enthusiastic neophyte, says: " 'We discuss everything and everyone – we're always discussing each other. . . . But don't you think it's the most interesting sort of talk?' " (125). At the same time (one makes the other possible), these displays of dirty linen can only come about because things are never called by their right names but are merely evoked or suggested. Thus this sentence with the force of law from the lips of Mrs. Brook: " 'Explanations, after all, spoil things' " (164); thus too her distress when she has to be explicit: " 'it's awfully vulgar to be talking about it, but . . . ' " (239). Mitchy observes in turn that the harder a topic is to mention, the more refined the conversation becomes. " 'The worse things are, . . . the better they seem positively to be for one's feeling up in the language' " (68). Language par excellence is like that of the Delphic oracle, which neither speaks nor keeps silent, but suggests. This constant requirement is however in contradiction with the objective of the main activity of all these characters, which, as we have seen, is nothing so much as asking for explanations. It is as if the characters were animated by two opposing forces, and participated simultaneously in two processes with competing values; motivated on the one hand by nostalgia for a direct hold on things, they try to see through words, to get around them in order to get hold of truth; but on the other hand, the possible failure of this quest is neutralized, as it were, by the pleasure they take in not stating the truth, in condemning it forever to uncertainty.

One of the principal events recounted in *The Awkward Age* is precisely the discomfort created in this salon through the upsetting but inevitable intervention in the salon of Mrs. Brook's daughter. Nanda had passed the age of childhood and thus has the right to come downstairs into the salon, but she has not yet reached the age of womanhood, so she must not hear everything. She herself, at first, perceives only the positive side of the event. " 'Now I shall be down. . . . Always. I shall see all the people who come. It will be a great thing for me. I want to hear all the talk. Mr. Mitchett says I ought to – that it helps to form the young mind' " (123). But her mother sees only the negative aspect of this intrusion: it will mean people have to speak less freely, it will dampen their conversation, and what is more precious than that? This is the feeling she expresses in a somewhat more complicated fashion to Mr. Cashmore: " 'She [Nanda] feels that her presence makes a difference in one's liberty of talk' " (137), and, more bluntly, to Vanderbank: " 'I spoke of the change in my life, of course. It happens to be so constituted that my life has something to do with my mind, and my mind something to do with my talk. Good talk: you know . . . what part, for me, that plays. Therefore when one has deliberately to make one's talk bad – . . . I mean stupid, flat, fourth-rate. When one has to take in sail to that degree – and for a perfectly outside reason – there's nothing strange in one's taking a friend sometimes into the confidence of one's irritation' " (237). After the fact, Nanda perceives the situation differently: " 'Doesn't one become a sort of a little drain-pipe with everything flowing through?' 'Why don't you call it more gracefully,' Mitchy asked, freshly struck, 'a little aeolian-harp set in the drawing-room window and vibrating in the breeze of conversation?' " (299–300). And in more direct language with Vanderbank: her mother, she says, feared " 'what we might pick up among you all that wouldn't be good for us' " (325); " 'the danger of picking up' " (ibid.).

In his preface, written ten years after the book itself, Henry James explained that this conflict and tension were at the very origin of the novel. "*The Awkward Age* is precisely a study of one of those curtailed or extended periods of tension and apprehension, an account of the manner in which the resented interference with ancient liberties came to be in a particular instance dealt with," "the case of the account to be taken, in a circle of free talk, of a new and innocent, a wholly unacclimatised presence," the story of "the freedom menaced by the inevitable irruption of the ingenious mind."[2] However, this origin, as he recognized in the same preface, is obscured – to the point of passing unnoticed – by what was initially intended to be only a form for that subject, a way of treating and elaborating it. But, as he remarks at the same time, "my subject was probably condemned in advance to appreciable... over-treatment" (1134). Nevertheless, "over-treatment" is never really possible (James calls this "an important artistic truth" [1135] arising ultimately out of his own experience). "The better lesson of my retrospect would seem to be really a supreme revision of the question of what it may be for a subject to suffer, to call it suffering, by over-treatment.... My artistic conscience meets the relief of having to recognise truly here no traces of suffering" (1137). Is it because this treatment can become a subject, and the subject can become a way of treating?

This form or manner of treating the subject – which is the tension created in conversation – is nothing but a series of conversations. *The Awkward Age* has one peculiarly distinguishing characteristic within the vast family of novels, namely that it is written almost entirely in dialogue. In other words, this novel closely resembles a drama, a genre that always fascinated Henry James. In his preface he offered a clear explanation of the use he sought to make of dialogue. The ideal he was after was "to make the presented occasion tell all its story itself, remain shut up in its own presence and yet on that patch of staked-out ground become thoroughly interesting and remain thoroughly clear..." (1132). Now is this not just what dramatic form offers? "The divine distinction of the act of a play... was, I reasoned, in its special, its guarded objectivity. This objectivity, in turn, when achieving its ideal, came from the imposed absence of that 'going behind,' to compass explanations and amplifications, to drag out odds and ends from the 'mere' storyteller's great property-shop of aids to illusion..." (1131).

[2] Henry James, preface to the New York edition of the *The Awkward Age,* in *Henry James: Literary Criticism* (New York: Literary Classics of the United States [Library of America], 1984) vol. I, 1124, 1122, 1124.

What draws James to the dialogue form is its objectivity, the possibility of getting along without any narrator, or at least without a narrator who knows and explains. It may be objected that *The Awkward Age* does have a narrator. We are reminded of his existence roughly every ten pages: he is a "spectator," and "observer" or "listener," described according to circumstances as "aware," "sharp," or "attentive." Sometimes this spectator is evoked in more detailed fashion: " 'an observer disposed to interpret the scene" (*The Awkward Age*, 108) who becomes "the ingenious observer just now suggested" (109) or "our sharp spectator" (111). Or else one supposes that "a person who knew him well would, if present at the scene, have found occasion in it to be freshly aware . . . " (197). Or one imagines "a quick turn of the glass that reflects the whole scene" (414). On other occasions, the narrator temporarily accepts the role of witness: "We should doubtless have gathered, had we seen . . . " (288) or, even more explicitly though in a negative way: "As Mr. Van himself could not have expressed, at any subsequent time, to any interested friend, the particular effect upon him of the tone of these words, his chronicler takes advantage of the fact not to pretend to a greater intelligence, to limit himself, on the contrary, to the simple statement that they produced in Mr. Van's cheek a just discernible flush" (176). At still other points, the narrator deplores the absence of such a witness: "Who was there to detect whether the girl observed it" (122), "[it] will never be known to history" (157). In every case this permanent witness, even if he is not constantly mentioned, remains indispensable and implicit in the presentation of events. The narrator, well aware of this, refers to "the acute observer we are *constantly* taking for granted," or "the *continuous* spectator of these episodes" (259, 432; emphasis added).

This witness who must be imagined (such a supposed presence led Dostoevsky to say that narratives of this sort are "fantastic," since they recognize the existence of invisible beings) nevertheless does not become a unifying narrative element; the narrator sees but does not know. It may be remarked that the characters themselves already have one curious habit (which contributes moreover to the difficulty of understanding their remarks and provokes requests for explanation): they do not refer to others by stable names known to all, but use expressions that vary from one situation to the next, as if they did not want to make any assumptions about the existence of an immutable identity within each being, but were content to register their perceptions, always specific to the occasion and subject to change. Thus in speaking to Mitchy about Carrie Donner, Mr. Cashmore's presumed mistress, the duchess calls her at one point " 'that preposterous little person' " (89); further on " 'the charming example of Mr. Cashmore's fine taste that we have there before us' " (91); still later " 'that victim of unjust aspersions' " (92), but she never calls her by her real name: poor Mrs. Donner has trouble existing as an entity. Characters become unstable, then, not only in passing from one moment to another but from one person's viewpoint to another. This is what leads to Nanda's remark: " 'We're . . . partly the result of other people' " (192), and Vanderbank's: " 'We see ourselves reflected' " (253). The narrator himself has adopted the same approach: he does not give his characters uniform names.

It is Vanderbank in one place, old Van in another, Mr. Van on still another occasion, depending on who is perceiving the character and under what circumstances, for the narrator himself has no perception that is specifically his own. In fact, the characters do all the perceiving, even when the narrator is speaking. Mrs. Brook becomes "the subject of this eulogy" (248) following a remark by Vanderbank, " 'Nanda's companion' " (264), in the course of a conversation with her daughter. Mr. Cashmore is on one occasion envisaged in relation to his wife, when he is called "her ladyship's husband" (134) and then in relation to his hostess, when he is "Mrs. Brook's visitor" (135). In the course of Mitchy's responses to Mr. Longdon (whose attention to names we have already noted), the latter is "the subject of Vanderbank's information" (102), then "old Van's possible confidant" (103); conversing with Vanderbank, Mr. Longdon becomes "Lady Julia's lover" (121); with Mrs. Brookenham, "the elder of her visitors" (144).

We may acknowledge that in this way each "presented occasion tell[s] all its story itself." But, even if the encounter remains "thoroughly interesting," it is not certain to be at the same time "thoroughly clear." To return to our starting point, even on a second reading we have some difficulty in reconstructing this story accurately, even in listing its main events, and there is probably no one who can spell out the exact nature of the relationships between Vanderbank and Mrs. Brook, Vanderbank and Nanda, Nanda and Mr. Longdon (to take only the principal characters).

There is a problem here that lies at the heart of this novel. The reader of any fictional text seeks to reconstruct the story the text is telling. Two types of information are available for this purpose. The first has to be inferred from the behaviors described; these behaviors then symbolize – but do not signify – the reality within the fiction. The second is provided directly by a narrator (or several). We know, however, that this narrator may prove "unreliable" in turn, and thus may oblige readers to infer the truth rather than to receive it directly. As *The Awkward Age* includes essentially no narratorial discourse, we may consider the characters themselves as so many narrators, and we need to be prepared to reestablish the truth even if they distort it. Now it is precisely in this task that the reader fails. Why?

Let us set aside first of all an obvious answer that does not apply here, according to which we are given mere talk while the action takes place elsewhere. So far as one can judge, no important event occurs during the periods of time that the book passes over in silence, nor does anything happen in the course of these time periods that would be situated outside of language, in nonverbal actions. Talk constitutes the principal events of the characters' lives, and their world is truly verbal. Did not James write in *The Question of Our Speech:* "It is very largely by saying, all the while, that we live and play our parts"[3]? Thus we must add, first of all, that no character accepts the role of narrator, even temporarily, in order to synthesize what has just happened.

---

[3] Henry James, *The Question of our Speech and The Lesson of Balzac: Two Lectures* (Boston and New York: Houghton Mifflin and Company, 1905) 21.

Not only is the novel made up of conversations, but these are quite peculiar conversations: they do not evoke events external to themselves, they *are* events. It is as though language-as-narrative and language-as-action were no longer complementary aspects of a single activity: in this story, conversations "tell" nothing at all. Conversations form the story but do not recount it.

But we still have not gone quite far enough. What one imagines as the underlying outline of this story – Nanda and Mrs. Brook both in love with Vanderbank, the latter poor, wanting to marry a wealthy woman but one whom he can love, the evolution of Mr. Longdon's feelings for Nanda – all this takes shape right before our eyes and yet we have the feeling that we are only granted indirect glimpses. This is not simply because, as we have amply noted, the rules of this society preclude naming things and allow them merely to be suggested. The problem is more fundamental, and it is what justifies the fact that this difficulty is at once the theme of the conversations and the principle according to which the novel is constructed. We have been led step by step from the simplest cases, where indirect expressions gave us direct access to solid and direct meanings, to vague words whose meaning can be grasped but which can never be interpreted with certainty. The novel contains facts and actions that we can reconstitute without a moment's hesitation, but at the same time it includes others – and for this reason alone perhaps they strike us as the most important – that will never be *established*. Obliqueness has attained such a degree that it is no longer obliqueness: the tethers between words and things have not only been loosened or twisted, they have been cut. Language functions in a space that will remain forever linguistic.

It is not that the characters lack sincerity, or that they do not attempt to formulate opinions about anything or anyone. They do try; and yet we cannot trust their words, for we have been surreptitiously deprived of a standard for measuring truth. Mr. Longdon finds truth difficult to express, and he is not alone. The indirect remarks exchanged by the characters have swept us along with a momentum whose power leaves far behind the allusions which served as its point of departure. Each remark turns out to be ontologically suspect, as it were, and we no longer know whether it leads to any reality, and if so, which one. Symbolization and inference might be bearers of solid information in a world where they found themselves framed by direct speech, or at least by instruments allowing interpretation to be oriented and verified. Yet – and herein lies James's technical prowess in *The Awkward Age* – indirect information is not only predominant in this book, it is the only information available. As it achieves its highest possible degree, it changes nature, and ceases to be information at all. The reader is thus implicated more deeply than ever in the construction of the fiction, and yet he discovers along the way that this construction can never be completed.

The relation of language to the world is ambiguous, and so too is Henry James's position with respect to this relation. Somewhere within himself he writes – as he always does – a social and realist novel, about love and money, thus about marriage. But words do not grasp things. Far from suffering from this, however – and in this he resembles his own characters, for *The Awkward Age* taken as a whole becomes an allegory of the creation of fiction – James gives himself over little by little to the pleasure he discovers in these sentences that give rise to others, ad infinitum; in these characters who provoke, seemingly all by themselves, the appearance of their doubles or their contraries; in these actions, born of symmetry and proportion. He who plays with words will have only words: this observation is tinged in James with two opposing feelings, regret at having lost the world, joy at the autonomous proliferation of language. And his novels are the incarnation of this ambiguity.

Proust too relates, in *Remembrance of Things Past,* how his characters discover that words do not necessarily tell the truth. But his discovery (that the direct language of words is inadequate) serves only to induce a happy awareness of the expressive power of the language of the body, or of what replaces this language in the verbal domain: figurative and indirect language. The deceptiveness of surfaces is compensated in Proust by the happiness procured through access to the depths. Indirect language is the only truthful language – but that is already saying a great deal, for then at least truth exists. The resemblance between Proust and James is thus misleading: we know perfectly well that the characters' discourse in *The Awkward Age* is indirect, but we never reach an underlying truth. Here the deceptive surface does refer to something else (it is in this that language is indirect), but that something else is still a surface, itself subject to interpretation. James does not lead us toward a new interiority, as Proust or Joyce do after him, but toward the absence of any interiority, thus toward the abolition of the very oppositions between inside and outside, between truth and appearance.

The entire construction of *The Awkward Age* (and not only that of the characters) rests on obliqueness, on *indirectness,* as if indirectness incarnated what is no longer the rule of a particular social group but the rule, period: indirectness always already prevails. In his preface, James recounts the project as follows: "I drew on a sheet of paper . . . the neat figure of a circle consisting of a number of small rounds disposed at equal distance about a central object. The central object was my situation, my subject in itself, to which the thing would owe its title, and the small rounds represented so many distinct lamps, as I liked to call them, the function of each of which would be to light with all due intensity one of its aspects. I had divided it . . . into aspects . . . Each of my 'lamps' would be the light of a single 'social occasion' in the history and intercourse of the characters concerned, and would bring out to the full the latent colour of the scene in question and cause it to illustrate, to the last drop, its bearing on my theme" (1130–1).

In reality things are a little more complicated. The novel is divided into thirty-eight chapters, each of which corresponds to a theatrical scene: the same characters engage in conversation from beginning to end. But over and above this division another is grafted, in ten books; these books, similar to the acts of a play, are characterized by unity of place, time (somewhat less tightly), and especially action (they have titles). Their titles are names of characters:

not necessarily one of the participants in the conversation (for example, the first book is called "Lady Julia," yet that character does not appear), but rather those who turn out to be, indirectly, illuminated by the conversation and who in turn determine its course. These ten character-books illuminate, finally, the central subject signaled by the title, "the awkward age." Thus we are in the presence of a perfect solar system (James speaks indeed of light): a center, ten large bodies arrayed around it, each one orbited by three or four satellite chapters. But this solar system has a startling peculiarity that reverses the meaning of the comparison: instead of emanating from the center toward the periphery, the light follows the opposite path. The satellites illuminate the planets, and these reflect the light, already indirect, back toward the sun. This sun thus remains quite dark, and the "subject in itself" imperceptible.

We may admire the infinite interpenetration of all the elements that form the system of the novel, and James himself, as a faithful though belated representative of the Romantic aesthetic, described the results of his work in his preface thus: "In doing this then it does more – it helps us ever so happily to see the grave distinction between substance and form in a really wrought work of art signally break down. . . . They are separate before the fact, but the sacrament of execution indissolubly marries them . . . The thing 'done,' artistically, is a fusion, or it has not *been* done . . . Prove this value, this effect, in the air of the whole result, to be of my subject, and that other value, other effect, to be of my treatment, prove that I haven't so shaken them together as the conjurer I profess to be *must* consummately shake, and I consent but to parade as before a booth at the fair" (1135–6). What could conceivably be more harmonious than this study of discourse carried out through the very use of discourse, this allusive manner of evoking allusion, this oblique book on obliqueness?

I believe *The Awkward Age* is one of the most important novels of our "age" and an exemplary book. But I believe this not only – not even primarily – because of the perfect fusion of "form" and "content," which many other works also achieve, and which we admire without ever quite knowing why. I would compare this book rather with the great novels that have followed it and that our modernity venerates much more, by virtue of the fact that it explores in depth a path opened up by language but unknown to literature, that it pushes this exploration further than had ever been done before or than has been done since. *The Awkward Age* is an exemplary book for representing – rather than declaring – the obliqueness of language and the undecidability of the world. This is one way of answering the question raised at the outset: What is *The Awkward Age* about? It is about what it means to talk, and to talk about something.

Index